Praise for *Running Lean, Second Edition*

"Easily one of the best technical books on Lean Startup ever written. Period. End of point. Done."

Dan Martell
Founder, Clarity.fm
Angel Investor

"In Running Lean, Ash has put together a book I wish I'd read before pursuing my own startup. The Lean methodology has received a lot of press, but the level of detail, including case studies and practical applications, make this book a resource worthy of sitting on every aspiring entrepreneur's shelf. It's not just great advice, but a great read, too."

Rand Fishkin
CEO and Cofounder, SEOmoz
Coauthor, *The Art of SEO*

"Customer validation has always been one of the best ways to eliminate wasted effort and shortcut directly to what will work. Eric Ries and Steve Blank did the startup world a great service by codifying and labeling the principles involved. Ash Maurya goes one step further, providing a clear roadmap for Internet entrepreneurs, with a delightfully clear and simple writing style."

David Skok
Author, For Entrepreneurs Blog
General Partner, Matrix Partners

"Ash provides compelling, actionable guidance for applying Lean principles to a startup. His startup canvas changed the way I think about my own startup. This book is a valuable guide whether you are a serial entrepreneur or a first-time founder."

Sean Ellis
Founder and CEO, CatchFree

"Running Lean *is the Missing Manual to the Lean Methodology that focuses on actionable tactics to help you find and vet your web startup idea. If you're considering building an application using the Lean methodology, you are wasting valuable time by not following the path Ash has laid out in this book."*

Rob Walling
Serial Entrepreneur
Author, *Start Small, Stay Small: A Developer's Guide to Launching a Startup*

Running Lean

Second Edition

Iterate from Plan A to a Plan That Works

Ash Maurya

O'REILLY®

Beijing · Cambridge · Farnham · Köln · Sebastopol · Tokyo

Running Lean, Second Edition
by Ash Maurya

Published by O'Reilly Media, Inc., 1005 Gravenstein Highway North, Sebastopol, CA 95472.

O'Reilly books may be purchased for educational, business, or sales promotional use. Online editions are also available for most titles (*http://safaribooksonline.com*). For more information, contact our corporate/institutional sales department: (800) 998-9938 or *corporate@oreilly.com*.

Editor: Mary Treseler

Production Editor: Holly Bauer

Copyeditor: Audrey Doyle

Proofreader: Kiel Van Horn

Indexer: Ellen Troutman Zaig

Production Services: Octal Publishing, Inc.

Cover Designer: Mark Paglietti

Interior Designer: Ron Bilodeau

Illustrators: Robert Romano, Rebecca Demarest, and Emiliano Villarreal

February 2011: First Edition.
February 2012: Second Edition.

Revision History for the Second Edition:

2012-11-02	Third release
2013-04-19	Fourth release
2013-08-23	Fifth release
2013-12-02	Sixth release
2014-03-07	Seventh release
2014-05-23	Eighth release
2014-07-25	Ninth release
2014-09-26	Tenth release
2014-11-14	Eleventh release

See *http://oreilly.com/catalog/errata.csp?isbn=0636920020141* for release details.

ISBN: 978-1-449-30517-8
[CW]

*For Natalia and Ian, who gave me a new appreciation
for our scarcest resource—time*

Contents

PART 4: SYSTEMATICALLY TEST YOUR PLAN

Foreword

Running Lean is the first book in the new *Lean Series*. Following the publication of *The Lean Startup* last year, I have had the opportunity to meet thousands of entrepreneurs and managers around the world. I have enjoyed hearing their stories and grappling with their questions. Most of all, I have heard an overwhelming demand for practical guidance for how to put Lean Startup principles into practice. There is no better person to begin that mission than Ash Maurya.

"Practice trumps theory." When I first read those words on Ash Maurya's blog, I knew he would be a valuable addition to a fledgling movement that was just getting started. Since then, he has been a tireless advocate for the Lean Startup movement. He has rigorously tested techniques for applying these ideas in his own startups, sharing what works and what doesn't. He has conducted countless workshops, each of which is a crucible for discovering the challenges that real entrepreneurs face and for evaluating which solutions really work. And he has been a leader in bringing the movement to his hometown of Austin, one of our most important startup hubs.

The result of all of this work is the volume you now hold in your hand. *Running Lean* is a handbook for practicing entrepreneurs who want to increase their odds of success. This is not a book of philosophy, or an entertaining compendium of anecdotes. Rather, it is a detailed look at a battle-tested approach to building companies that matter.

We are living in an age of entrepreneurship. Most of the net new job growth in the USA in the past few decades has come from high-growth startups. All of us—investors, managers, policy makers, and ordinary citizens—have an interest in creating the conditions that will foster entrepreneurship. Our future prosperity depends on it.

There are probably more entrepreneurs operating today than at any time in history, thanks to profound changes in the startup landscape. New technologies, like cloud computing, are making it easier and cheaper to get started. New management methods, like the Lean Startup, are helping founders make better use of these capabilities. There has never been a better time to be an entrepreneur.

If I had to summarize these changes in one phrase, it would be this one: "the rentership of the means of production"—turning Karl Marx's famous dictum on its head. In past eras, to build and operate a company of significant scale required dozens of stakeholders to give you permission. You needed access to capital, machinery, factories, warehouses, distribution partners, mass-market advertising, and so on.

Today, anyone with a credit card can *rent* all of these capabilities and more. What is significant about this development is that it enables more startup experiments than ever before. And make no mistake, a startup *is* an experiment. Today's companies can build anything they can imagine. So the question we are called on to answer is no longer primarily, "*can* it be built?", but rather, "*should* it be built?"

We need these experiments more than ever. The old management tools, pioneered by 20th-century companies like General Motors, relied on planning and forecasting in order to measure progress, assess opportunities, and hold managers accountable. And yet who really feels that our world is getting more and more stable every day?

Successful new products require constant, disciplined, experimentation—in the scientific sense—in order to discover new sources of profitable growth. This is true for the tiniest startup as well as for the most established company.

Running Lean provides a step-by-step blueprint to put these ideas into action. A business plan rests on a series of leap-of-faith assumptions, each of which can be tested empirically. Will customers want the product we're building? Will they pay for it? Can we provide a service profitably? And once we find customers, can we grow? *Running Lean* lays out Ash's approach to breaking these assumptions down so that they can become the subjects of rigorous experiments.

Running Lean's simple, action-oriented templates provide tools that startups in all stages of development can use to help build breakthrough, disruptive new products and organizations.

It's been just about three years since I first wrote the phrase "lean startup" in a blog post that a few dozen people read. Since then, these ideas have grown into a movement, embraced by thousands of entrepreneurs around the world dedicated to making sure that new products and new startups succeed. As you read through *Running Lean*, I hope you will put these ideas into practice and join our community. Odds are there is a Lean Startup Meetup taking place in your city. A complete list of meetups and links to other resources can be found at the official Lean Startup homepage: *http://theleanstartup.com*.

Welcome to the cutting edge of entrepreneurial practice. I hope you'll share what you learn, what works and what doesn't. Thank you for being part of this experiment.

Eric Ries
January 20, 2012
San Francisco, CA

Preface

The first edition of *Running Lean* (released as an ebook) was targeted primarily at people like me: technical founders building web-based products. I was running my first company and on my fifth product at the time. I had been inspired by Steve Blank's book *The Four Steps to the Epiphany* (*http://www.cafepress.com/kandsranch*) and the early works on the Lean Startup methodology by Eric Ries.

My goal with the ebook was to create an actionable guide for other entrepreneurs building web-based products. I wrote and self-published the ebook iteratively using the same methodology outlined in the ebook.

However, once the ebook was published in January 2011, the audience for the book grew beyond my prototypical early adopter, and I was repeatedly met with two kinds of feedback:

- "I can see how these techniques worked for your business, but they won't work for me because I am building X."

- "Even though I am building X, these techniques have greatly helped my business with only slight modifications."

(Where X ranged from software to hardware, B2C to B2B, and high-tech to low-tech.)

I was curious and decided to explore further. In the past year, I have actively sought opportunities to expose and test these ideas with a wide range of businesses by way of running workshops, taking on mentor positions at several accelerators, and working closely with other entrepreneurs. I still remember being nervous the first time I delivered a workshop to a room full of biotech entrepreneurs. But each time, the results were positively encouraging.

The second edition of *Running Lean* aims to synthesize my learning over the past year and broaden the audience. Even though a lot of these ideas came out of the high-tech startup world, I believe the principles they embody are universally applicable to any startup or product.

This is reflected in a completely new layout for the book that delineates meta-principles from tactics.

I have also replaced the Lean Canvas case study (which some people found confusing) with a more complete example that follows throughout the book from ideation to exit. In addition, I've supplemented the text with several other smaller case studies from a wide range of products that illustrate these principles at work.

Finally, since I wrote the first version, Eric Ries has published his book, *The Lean Startup* (Crown Business). Along with being the authoritative guide on Lean Startups, the book also introduces several new and powerful concepts like Innovation Accounting and Engines of Growth that I have incorporated into this edition.

Safari® Books Online

Safari Books Online is an on-demand digital library that lets you easily search over 7,500 technology and creative reference books and videos to find the answers you need quickly.

With a subscription, you can read any page and watch any video from our library online. Read books on your cell phone and mobile devices. Access new titles before they are available for print, and get exclusive access to manuscripts in development and post feedback for the authors. Copy and paste code samples, organize your favorites, download chapters, bookmark key sections, create notes, print out pages, and benefit from tons of other time-saving features.

O'Reilly Media has uploaded this book to the Safari Books Online service. To have full digital access to this book and others on similar topics from O'Reilly and other publishers, sign up for free at *http://safaribooksonline. com.*

We'd Like to Hear from You

Please address comments and questions concerning this book to the publisher:

O'Reilly Media, Inc.
1005 Gravenstein Highway North
Sebastopol, CA 95472
(800) 998-9938 (in the United States or Canada)
(707) 829-0515 (international or local)
(707) 829-0104 (fax)

We have a web page for this book, where we list errata, examples, and any additional information. You can access this page at:

http://shop.oreilly.com/product/0636920020141.do

To comment or ask technical questions about this book, send email to:

bookquestions@oreilly.com

For more information about our books, courses, conferences, and news, see our website at *http://www.oreilly.com*.

Find us on Facebook: *http://facebook.com/oreilly*

Follow us on Twitter: *http://twitter.com/oreillymedia*

Watch us on YouTube: *http://www.youtube.com/oreillymedia*

Attributions and Permissions

This book is here to help you get your job done. If you reference limited parts of it in your work or writings, we appreciate, but do not require, attribution. An attribution usually includes the title, author, publisher, and ISBN. For example: "*Running Lean, Second Edition* (O'Reilly). Copyright 2012 Ash Maurya, 978-1-449-30517-8."

If you feel your use of examples or quotations from this book falls outside fair use or the permission given above, feel free to contact us at *permissions@ oreilly.com*.

Introduction

What Is Running Lean?

We live in an age of unparalleled opportunity for innovation. With the advent of the Internet, cloud computing, and open source software, the cost of building products is at an all-time low. Yet, the odds of building successful startups haven't improved much.

Most startups still fail.

But the more interesting fact is that, of those startups that succeed, two-thirds report having drastically changed their plans along the way.[1]

So, what separates successful startups from unsuccessful ones is not necessarily the fact that successful startups began with a better initial plan (or Plan A), but rather that they *find a plan that works* before *running out of resources.*

Up until now, finding this better Plan B or C or Z has been based more on gut, intuition, and luck. There has been no systematic process for rigorously stress-testing a Plan A.

That is what Running Lean is about.

Running Lean is a systematic process for iterating from Plan A to a plan that works, before running out of resources.

Why Are Startups Hard?

First, there is a misconception around how successful products get built. The media loves stories of visionaries who see the future and chart a perfect course to intersect it. The reality, however, rarely plays out quite as simply. Even the unveiling of the visionary computer, the iPad, in Steve Jobs' words

---

1   John Mullins and Randy Komisar, *Getting to Plan B* (Boston, MA: Harvard Business Review Press, 2009).

was years in the making, built on several incremental innovations (and failures) of software and hardware.

Second, the classic product-centric approach front-loads some customer involvement during the requirements-gathering phase but leaves most of the customer validation until after the software is released. There is a large "middle" when the startup disengages from customers for weeks or months while they build and test their solution. During this time, it's quite possible for the startup to either build too much or be led astray from building what customers want. This is the fundamental dilemma described by Steve Blank in *The Four Steps to the Epiphany*, in which he offers a process for building a continuous customer feedback loop throughout the product development cycle that he terms "Customer Development."

And finally, even though customers hold all the answers, you simply cannot ask them what they want.

> *If I had asked people what they wanted, they would have said faster horses.*
>
> —*Henry Ford*

A lot of people cite the preceding quote and declare it hopeless to talk to customers. But hidden in this quote is a customer problem statement: had customers said "faster horses," they would really have been asking for something *faster* than their existing alternative, which happened to be horses.

Given the right context, customers can clearly articulate their problems, but it's your job to come up with the solution.

> *It is not the customer's job to know what they want.*
>
> —*Steve Jobs*

Is There a Better Way?

Running Lean provides a better, faster way to vet new product ideas and build successful products:

- Running Lean is about speed, learning, and focus.

- Running Lean is about testing a vision by measuring how customers behave.

- Running Lean is about engaging customers throughout the product development cycle.

- Running Lean tackles both product and market validation in parallel using short iterations.

- Running Lean is a disciplined and rigorous process.

Running Lean references an array of methodologies and thinkers. Three of the most important follow.

Customer Development

Customer Development is a term coined by Steve Blank and is used to describe the parallel process of building a continuous feedback loop with customers throughout the product development cycle. It is defined in his book, *The Four Steps to the Epiphany*.

The key takeaway from Customer Development can best be summed up as:

> *Get out of the building.*
>
> —*Steve Blank*

Most of the answers lie outside the building—not on your computer, or in the lab. You have to get out and directly engage customers.

Lean Startup

Lean Startup is a term trademarked by Eric Ries and represents a synthesis of Customer Development, Agile Software Development methodologies, and Lean (as in the Toyota Production System) practices.

The term *Lean* is often misunderstood as "being cheap." While "being Lean" is fundamentally about eliminating waste or being efficient with resources, that interpretation is not completely misguided because money happens to be one of those resources.

However, in a Lean Startup, we strive to optimize utilization of our scarcest resource, which is time. Specifically, our objective is *maximizing learning (about customers) per unit time*.

The key takeaway from Lean Startup can best be summed up around the concept of using smaller, faster iterations for testing a vision.

> *Startups that succeed are those that manage to iterate enough times before running out of resources.*
>
> —*Eric Ries*

Bootstrapping

Bootstrapping is more commonly understood as a collection of techniques used to minimize the amount of external debt or funding needed from banks or investors. Too often, people confuse bootstrapping with self-funding. A stricter definition is funding with customer revenues.

However, I subscribe to a much more philosophical definition of bootstrapping put forward by Bijoy Goswami:

Right action, right time.

Startups are inherently chaotic, but at any given point in time, there are only a few key actions that matter. You need to just focus on those and ignore the rest.

What Will This Book Teach You?

In this book, you'll learn:

- How to first find a problem worth solving, before defining a solution
- How to find early customers
- When is the ideal time to raise funding
- How to test pricing
- How to decide what goes into Release 1.0
- How to build and measure what customers want
- How to maximize for speed, learning, and focus
- What is product/market fit
- How to iterate to product/market fit

Is This Book for You?

If you are an entrepreneur considering building a new product, or if you already have a product and you want to raise your odds of making it successful, this book is for you.

Running Lean is for:

- Business managers
- CEOs
- Developers and programmers who are interested in becoming successful entrepreneurs
- Bloggers, cofounders, small-business people, writers, musicians— anyone who's creative and interested in starting a new business project
- Innovators
- Startup founders

How Is This Book Organized?

This book is organized into four parts. The parts are meant to be read in order, as they outline the chronological steps required to apply Running Lean to your product—from ideation to product/market fit. Even if you already have a product launched, I recommend starting from the beginning. You will not have to spend as much time going through the stages, and this exercise will help you baseline where you currently are and formulate your next actions.

Each part ends with gating criteria that will help you decide if you're ready to move on to the next one.

Part 1: Roadmap

Part 1 provides an overall roadmap of the Running Lean process. Specifically, it describes the three core meta-principles that capture the essence of Running Lean and ends with a short case study that helps illustrate these principles in action.

The rest of the book covers each of the following meta-principles in detail in three parts.

Part 2: Document Your Plan A

Part 2 walks through the process of documenting your initial vision (or Plan A) using a portable one-page format called Lean Canvas. Your Lean Canvas will serve as your product's tactical map and blueprint.

Part 3: Identify the Riskiest Parts of Your Plan

Part 3 helps you identify which aspects of your plan to focus on first. It lays some groundwork on the different types of risks startups face, shows you how to prioritize them, and prepares you to start the process of testing and experimentation.

Part 4: Systematically Test Your Plan

Part 4 outlines the four-stage process for systematically stress testing your initial plan and shows you how to iterate from your Plan A to a Plan That Works.

About Me

I bootstrapped my most recent company, WiredReach, in 2002, and sold it in late 2010. Throughout that time, I built products in stealth, attempted building a platform, dabbled with open sourcing, practiced "release early, release often," embraced "less is more,"[2] and even tried "more is more."

The first realization early on was that building in stealth is a really bad idea. There is a fear, especially common among first-time entrepreneurs, that their great idea will be stolen by someone else. The truth is twofold: first, most people are not able to visualize the potential of an idea at such an early stage, and second (and more importantly), *they won't care.*

The second realization was that startups can *consume years of your life.* I started WiredReach with just a spark of an idea, and before I knew it, years had passed. While I've had varying levels of success with the products I built, I realized that I needed a better, faster way to vet new product ideas.

Life's too short to build something nobody wants.

And finally, I learned that while listening to customers is important, *you have to know how to do it.* I used a "release early, release often" methodology for one of my products, BoxCloud, and launched a fairly minimal file-sharing product built on a new peer-to-web model we had developed in 2006. After we launched, we got covered by a few prominent blogs and dumped some serious cash into advertising on the DECK network (primarily targeted at designers and developers).

We started getting a lot of feedback from users, but it was all over the place. We didn't have a clear definition of our target customer and didn't know how to prioritize this feedback. We started listening to the most popular (vocal) requests and ended up with a bloated application and lots of one-time-use features.

Around that time, I ran into Steve Blank's lectures on Customer Development, from which I followed the trail to Eric Ries's early ideas of the Lean Startup. I had dreamt the big vision, rationalized it in my head, and built it and refined it the long, hard way. I knew customers held the answers but didn't know when or how to fully engage them. That's exactly what Customer Development and Lean Startup were attempting to address.

I was sold.

---

2 A product development philosophy popularized by 37signals.

Why This Book?

I was determined to test these techniques on my next product (CloudFire) but ran into many early challenges when trying to take these concepts to practice.

For one, Steve Blank's book was written for a specific type of business, enterprise software, which made it hard to carry over many of the tactics to my products. Also, while Eric Ries was sharing his retrospective lessons learned from working at IMVU, IMVU was no longer a startup. With a technical staff of 40 people and more than $40 million in revenue, what you saw was a fully realized Lean Startup machine, which was at times daunting.

I had more questions than answers, which prompted my two-year journey in search of a better methodology for building successful products. The product of that journey is *Running Lean*, which is based on my firsthand experiential learning building products and the pioneering work of Eric Ries, Steve Blank, Dave McClure, Sean Ellis, Sean Murphy, Jason Cohen, Alex Osterwalder, and many others who I reference throughout the book.

I am thankful to the thousands of readers who subscribed to my blog, left comments week after week, sent me notes of encouragement to keep on writing, and subjected their products to my testing. This book was really "pulled" out of me by them.

Field-Tested

As a way to test the content for this book, I started speaking and teaching Running Lean workshops. I have shared this methodology with hundreds of startups and worked closely with many of them to test and refine it.

Whereas my blog is a near-real-time account of my lessons learned, this book benefits from retrospective learning and from reordering and refining steps for a more optimal workflow.

I am applying this new workflow to my next startup, which is also a by-product of my blogging and learning over the past year. As of this writing, I have sold WiredReach and am in the process of building and launching a new startup, Spark59.

Disclaimers

Practice Trumps Theory

You get a gold star not for following a process, but for achieving results. One of the things that particularly drew me to the Lean Startup methodology is that it is a meta-process from which more specific processes and practices can be formulated. The same principles used to test your product can and should be applied to test your tactics when taking these principles to practice.[3]

Everything in this book is based on first-hand experiential learning and experimentation on my own products. I encourage you to rigorously test and adapt these principles for yourself. The legal, financial, and accounting aspects of launching a company are outside the scope of the book. When the time comes, it is important to get competent professional advice about financing and structuring your company and its intellectual property assets.

There Are No Silver Bullets

No methodology can guarantee success. But a good methodology can provide a feedback loop for continuous improvement and learning.

That is the promise of this book.

---

3   There is no room for faith in a Lean Startup: *http://www.ashmaurya.com/2011/02/do-you-have-faith-in-lean-startups/*.

PART 1

ROADMAP

Meta-Principles

The proper application of any methodology first requires a clear understanding and separation of principles from tactics.

Principles guide what you do. Tactics show you how.

The essence of Running Lean can be distilled into three steps:

1. Document your Plan A.

2. Identify the riskiest parts of your plan.

3. Systematically test your plan.

In this chapter, we'll cover these meta-principles. The rest of the book will focus on the reduction of these meta-principles to practice.

Step 1: Document Your Plan A

There Is an "I" in Vision

> *All men dream: but not equally. Those that dream by night in the dusty*
> *recesses of their minds wake in the day to find that it was vanity:*
> *but the dreamers of the day are dangerous men, for they may act*
> *their dreams with open eyes, to make it possible.*
>
> > —*T.E. Lawrence, "Lawrence of Arabia"*

Everyone gets hit by ideas when they least expect them (in the shower, while driving, etc.). Most people ignore them. Entrepreneurs choose to act on them.

While passion and determination are attributes that are essential in order to drive a vision to its full potential, if they are left unchecked, they can also turn the journey into a faith-based one driven by dogma.

Reasonably smart people can rationalize anything, but entrepreneurs are especially gifted at this.

Most entrepreneurs start with a strong initial vision and a Plan A for realizing that vision. Unfortunately, *most Plan A's don't work.*

While a strong vision is required to create a mantra and make meaning, a Lean Startup strives to uphold a strong vision with facts, not faith. It is important to accept that your initial vision is built largely on untested assumptions (or hypotheses). Running Lean helps you systematically test and refine that initial vision.

Capture Your Business Model Hypotheses

Too many founders carry their hypotheses in their heads alone, which, though the fastest way to iterate, only helps to further support their own "reality distortion fields."

The first step is *writing down* your initial vision and then *sharing* it with at least one other person.

Traditionally, business plans have been used for this purpose. But, while writing a business plan is a good exercise for the entrepreneur, it falls short of its true purpose: Facilitating conversations with people other than yourself.

Additionally, since most Plan As are likely to be proven wrong anyway, you need something less static and rigid than a business plan. Taking several weeks or months to write a 60-page business plan largely built on untested hypotheses is a form of waste.

> *Waste is any human activity which absorbs resources but creates no value.*
> —*James P. Womak and Daniel T. Jones,* Lean Thinking *(Free Press)*

My format of choice is to use the one-page business model diagram (Lean Canvas) shown in Figure 1-1.

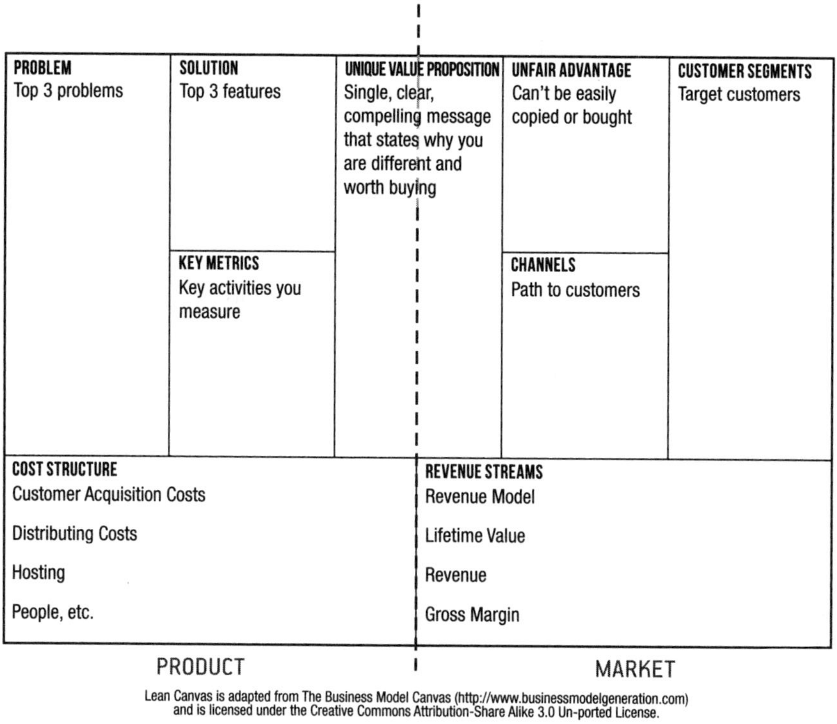

PROBLEM	SOLUTION	UNIQUE VALUE PROPOSITION	UNFAIR ADVANTAGE	CUSTOMER SEGMENTS
Top 3 problems	Top 3 features	Single, clear, compelling message that states why you are different and worth buying	Can't be easily copied or bought	Target customers
	KEY METRICS Key activities you measure		CHANNELS Path to customers	

COST STRUCTURE	REVENUE STREAMS
Customer Acquisition Costs Distributing Costs Hosting People, etc.	Revenue Model Lifetime Value Revenue Gross Margin

PRODUCT   MARKET

Lean Canvas is adapted from The Business Model Canvas (http://www.businessmodelgeneration.com)
and is licensed under the Creative Commons Attribution-Share Alike 3.0 Un-ported License.

Figure 1-1. *Lean Canvas*

Lean Canvas is my adaptation of Alex Osterwalder's Business Model Canvas, which he describes in the book *Business Model Generation* (Wiley).[1]

I particularly like the one-page canvas format because it is:

Fast

Compared to writing a business plan, which can take several weeks or months, you can outline multiple business models on a canvas in one afternoon. Because creating these one-page business models takes so little time, I recommend spending a little additional time up front, brainstorming possible variations to your model and then prioritizing where to start.

Concise

The canvas forces you to pick your words carefully and get to the point. This is great practice for distilling the essence of your product. You have 30 seconds to grab the attention of an investor over a

---

1 To understand the differences between Lean Canvas and the original Business Model Canvas, see *http://www.ashmaurya.com/why-lean-canvas*.

hypothetical elevator ride, and eight seconds to grab the attention of a customer on your landing page.[2]

Portable

A single-page business model is much easier to share with others, which means it will be read by more people and probably will be more frequently updated.

If you have ever written a business plan or created a slide deck for investors, you'll immediately recognize most of the building blocks on the canvas. I won't spend time describing these blocks right now, as we'll cover them in great detail in Part 2 of the book.

A key point I would like you to take away for now, though, is that *your product is NOT "the product"* of your startup.

Your Product Is NOT "the Product"

I purposely made the solution box less than one-ninth of the entire canvas because, as entrepreneurs, we are most passionate about the solution box and what we are naturally good at (see Figure 1-2).

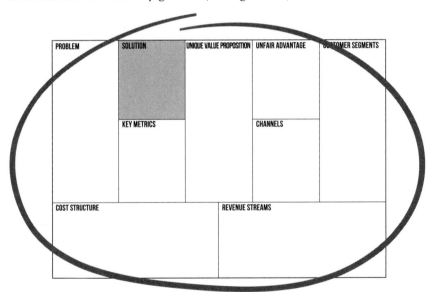

Your "business model" is the product

Lean Canvas is adapted from The Business Model Canvas (http://www.businessmodelgeneration.com)
and is licensed under the Creative Commons Attribution-Share Alike 3.0 Un-ported License.

Figure 1-2. *Your product is NOT "the product"*

---

2 It is estimated that up to 50% of visitors to landing pages will bail in the first eight seconds. Source: MarketingSherpa's "Landing Page Handbook" (2005).

CHAPTER 1

Dave McClure of 500 Startups has sat through hundreds of entrepreneur pitches and will probably sit through hundreds more. During these sessions, he has repeatedly called out entrepreneurs for spending a disproportionate amount of time talking about their solution and *not* enough time talking about the other components of the business model.

> *Customers don't care about your solution. They care about their problems.*
>
> —*Dave McClure, 500 Startups*

Investors, and more important, customers, identify with their problems and *don't care about your solution (yet)*. Entrepreneurs, on the other hand, are naturally wired to look for solutions. But chasing after solutions to problems no one cares enough about is a form of waste.

Your job isn't just building the best solution, but owning the entire business model and making all the pieces fit.

Recognizing your business model as a product is empowering. Not only does it let you own your business model, but it also allows you to apply well-known techniques from product development to building your company.

If you take a step back, you'll see that these meta-principles are nothing more than the *divide and conquer* technique applied to the process of starting up.

Lean Canvas helps deconstruct your business model into nine distinct subparts that are then systematically tested, in order of highest to lowest risk.

Step 2: Identify the Riskiest Parts of Your Plan

Building a successful product is fundamentally about risk mitigation.

Customers buy from you when they trust you can solve their problems. Investors bet on you when they trust you can build a scalable business model.

Startups are a risky business, and our real job as entrepreneurs is to systematically de-risk our startups over time.

Another technique taken from the Product Development playbook is that of "tackling the riskiest parts first." Not coincidentally, for most products, the solution isn't what's riskiest.

Unless you are trying to solve a particularly hard technical problem (like finding a cure for cancer, building the next big search algorithm, or splitting isotopes), chances are you will be able to build your product given enough time, money, and effort.

The bigger risk for most startups is building something nobody wants.

While what's riskiest varies across products, a lot of that risk is driven by the stage of your startup, which we'll cover next.

The Three Stages of a Startup

A startup goes through three distinct stages, as shown in Figure 1-3.

Figure 1-3. *Three stages of a startup*

Stage 1: Problem/Solution Fit

Key question: Do I have a problem worth solving?

The first stage is about determining whether you have a *problem worth solving* before investing months or years of effort into building a solution.

While ideas are cheap, acting on them is quite expensive.

A problem worth solving boils down to three questions:

- Is it something customers want? (must-have)
- Will they pay for it? If not, who will? (viable)
- Can it be solved? (feasible)

During this stage, we attempt to answer these questions using a combination of qualitative customer observation and interviewing techniques that we'll cover in great detail Chapters 5 and 6.[3]

From there you derive the minimum feature set to address the right set of problems, which is also known as the minimum viable product (MVP).

Stage 2: Product/Market Fit

Key question: Have I built something people want?

Once you have a problem worth solving and your MVP has been built, you then test how well your solution solves the problem. In other words, you measure whether you have built *something people want.*

---

3 In *The Four Steps to the Epiphany*, Steve Blank points out the importance of in-depth customer interviews, which he terms "Customer Discovery."

In Part 4 of this book, we'll cover both qualitative and quantitative metrics for measuring product/market fit.

Achieving traction or product/market fit is the first significant milestone for a startup. At this stage, you have a plan that is starting to work—you are signing up customers, retaining them, and getting paid.

Stage 3: Scale

Key question: How do I accelerate growth?

After product/market fit, some level of success is almost always guaranteed. Your focus at this stage shifts toward growth, or *scaling* your business model.

Pivot Before Product/Market Fit, Optimize After

Achieving product/market fit is the first significant milestone of a startup and greatly influences both strategy and tactics. For this reason, it is helpful to further delineate the stages of a startup as "before product/market fit" and "after product/market fit."

Before product/market fit, the focus of the startup centers on *learning and pivots*. After product/market fit, the focus shifts toward *growth and optimizations*. (See Figure 1-4.)

Figure 1-4. *Before and after product/market fit*

Pivot is a term used by Eric Ries to describe a change in direction of a startup while staying grounded in learning. The best way to differentiate pivots from optimizations is that pivots are about *finding a plan that works*, while optimizations are about *accelerating that plan*.

In a pivot experiment, you attempt to *validate* parts of the business model hypotheses in order to find a plan that works. In an optimization experiment, you attempt to *refine* parts of the business model hypotheses in order to accelerate a working plan. The goal of the first is a course correction (or a pivot). The goal of the second is efficiency (or scale).

This may sound like a subtle distinction, but it has a significant impact on both strategic and tactical execution. Before product/market fit, a startup needs to be architected to maximize learning.

You stand to learn the most when the probability of the expected outcome is 50%; that is, when you don't know what to expect.

In order to maximize learning, you have to *pick bold outcomes* instead of chasing incremental improvements. So, rather than changing the color of your call-to-action button, change your entire landing page. Rather than tweaking your unique value proposition (UVP) for a single customer segment, experiment with different UVPs for different customer segments.

Later in the book, we'll visit many other examples that explain how you purposely architect for learning over optimization.

Where Does Funding Fit into All This?

It's funny to note how the 37signals folks went from "Outside money is Plan B" to "Outside money is Plan Z" between their last two books: *Getting Real* and *Rework* (37signals.com). Once you're profitable, it's easy to make such a declaration, but some times are certainly better than others to consider external funding (see Figure 1-5).

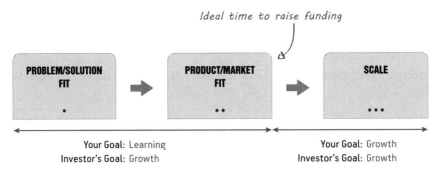

Figure 1-5. *Ideal time to raise funding*

Even though you may need to raise seed funding sooner, the ideal time to raise your big round of funding is *after product/market fit*, because at that time, both you and your investors have aligned goals: to scale the business.

> *Traction is a measure of your product's engagement with its market. Investors care about traction over everything else.*
> —Nivi and Naval, Venture Hacks

A lot of (especially first-time) entrepreneurs feel that Step 1 involves writing a business plan/building a slide deck and getting funded. Taking several months to write and pitch a business plan to investors is not the best use of time for a startup; especially since all you have at that point is a vision and a set of untested hypotheses. Selling this to investors without any level of validation is a form of waste.

Instead, your first goal should be to establish *just enough of a runway* to allow you to start testing and validating your business model with customers.

While not the same thing, bootstrapping and Lean Startups are quite complementary. Both cover techniques for building *low-burn startups* by eliminating waste through the *maximization of existing resources* before expending effort on the acquisition of new or external resources.

Bootstrapping + Lean Startup = Low-Burn Startup

(For more, see "How to Build a Low-Burn Startup" in the Appendix.)

Step 3: Systematically Test Your Plan

With your Plan A documented and your starting risks prioritized, you are now ready to systematically test your plan. In a Lean Startup, this is done by running a series of experiments.

The Lean Startup methodology is strongly rooted in the scientific method, and running experiments is a key activity. We'll cover steps for running effective experiments in Part 3 of the book, but for now, let's start by defining an experiment.

What Is an Experiment?

A cycle around the validated learning loop shown in Figure 1-6 is called an experiment.

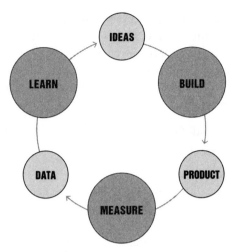

Figure 1-6. *Build-Measure-Learn loop*

The validated learning loop, or Build-Measure-Learn loop, was codified by Eric Ries and describes the customer feedback loop that drives learning in a Lean Startup.

It begins in the Build stage with a set of ideas or hypotheses that are used to create some artifact (mock-ups, code, landing page, etc.) for the purpose of testing a hypothesis. We put this artifact in front of customers and *"measure"* their response using a combination of qualitative and quantitative data. This data is used to derive specific *"learning"* that serves to validate or refute a hypothesis, which in turn drives the next set of actions.

The Iteration Meta-Pattern

While an experiment helps you validate or invalidate a specific business model hypothesis, an *iteration* strings multiple experiments together toward achieving a specific goal, such as getting to product/market fit.

Figure 1-7 shows the basic iteration meta-pattern we'll use throughout this book.

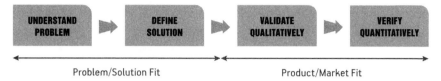

Figure 1-7. *Iteration meta-pattern*

The first two stages (Understand Problem and Define Solution) are about getting to problem/solution fit or finding a problem worth solving.

Then you iterate toward product/market fit by testing whether you've built something people want using a two-stage approach: first qualitative (micro-scale), then quantitative (macro-scale).

Running Lean Illustrated

A great way to understand the meta-principles covered in Chapter 1 is to see them applied to a real product.

I wanted to pick a simple example that would be readily understood. So, rather than picking a software or hardware product, I decided to outline the process I used to write this book.

Even if you haven't written a book, you can probably appreciate the steps that go into writing a book, which, as you'll see, isn't unlike building a product.

Case Study: How I ~~Wrote~~ Iterated This Book

Writing a book was never in my plans. I was too busy running my company. I started my blog in October 2009 because I had more questions about Lean Startups than answers.

Along the way, a few of my blog readers started suggesting that I turn my blog posts into a book. I knew writing a book (even from blog posts) would be a massive undertaking, so while I was flattered by the requests, *I did nothing at first*. After about a dozen such requests, I decided to explore further.

What follows is how I applied the Running Lean process to writing this book.

Understand the Problem

I called these readers and asked them why they wanted me to write a book. Specifically, I asked *what would be different* about this book from what was already on my blog, or in other blogs and books that are already out there. In other words, I was trying to understand this book's *unique value proposition* in relation to *existing alternatives.*

From these interviews, I learned that, like me, my readers were also struggling with taking Customer Development and Lean Startup techniques to practice (*problem statement*) and viewed my blog posts as a "step-by-step" guide for applying these techniques from the ground up (*solution*). Many of them were also technical founders like me who were building web-based products (*early adopters*).

Define the Solution

With that knowledge, I spent a day *building a demo*. It was a teaser landing page with a table of contents, a title, and a stock book-cover image (see Figure 2-1).

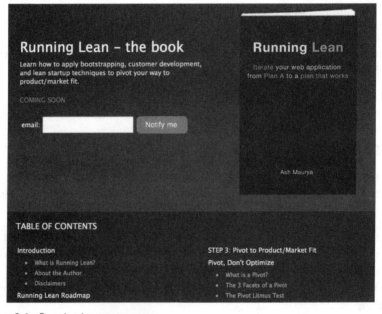

Figure 2-1. *Running Lean teaser page*

I knew the *riskiest part* about writing this book was nailing down the table of contents—not the title, book cover, or even price (since most business books have fairly established pricing).

I called the same readers and asked them: "If I were to write this book, would they buy it?" Their feedback helped me refine the table of contents (*define the solution*) and gave me a strong signal to move forward.

While encouraging, writing a book for just a dozen or so readers wasn't indicative of a *problem worth solving*. So I left the teaser page up and announced the book with a "coming this summer" launch time frame on my blog in March 2010. My readers helped spread the message (*channel testing*). Then I went back to running my company.

By June, I had collected 1,000 emails (*potential prospects*), which made writing the book a problem worth solving for me. My rationale for this was at least covering my costs using a simple back-of-the-envelope calculation.

Validate Qualitatively

Writing a whole book was still a massive undertaking. I tried writing the first chapter using "copy-and-paste" from my blog but wasn't happy with the results. I needed to build something even smaller that allowed me to start learning from customers (*a minimum viable product*).

I took the table of contents and turned it into a slide deck with the same outline and a few bullet points under each topic. I announced a free Running Lean workshop in Austin, Texas and got 30 people interested.

A local incubator, Tech Ranch, was gracious enough to provide a venue but only had room for 10 people. This was perfect, as it meant I could run at least two more workshops with the others (*iterate in small batches*).

Based on the success of the first workshop, not only did I run more workshops, but I also started charging for them (*getting paid is the first form of validation*). With each workshop, I continually tweaked the slide deck content for better flow and doubled pricing until I hit some resistance.

By the end of the summer, I understood the solution well enough and started writing. Here again, instead of writing the whole book in isolation, I contacted my potential prospects from the teaser page, many of whom were growing impatient as my initial launch date had come and gone. I apologized for not having finished the book and told them I'd be writing and releasing the book *iteratively*, much like software. Rather than waiting six more months to get the book, if they preordered the book, now they would get two chapters of the book every two weeks in PDF format.

About half of the people agreed to this arrangement. The others chose to wait for the "finished product," citing print, iPad, and/or Kindle as their preferred reading format. This further helped me distinguish *early adopters* from latter-stage customers. These early adopters were driven by the content alone and didn't care how it was packaged. The content for me was still the riskiest part of the product to test.

Customer feedback during this two-week iteration cycle was immensely valuable. Entire chapters were rewritten for better flow, illustrations were improved,[1] and little typos and grammatical errors were nipped in the bud. Not only was I able to write a *better* book using this process, but I did so *faster*.

Verify Quantitatively

Only once the book was "content-complete" in January 2011 did I hire a designer for the book cover, start testing book subtitles, research print/ ebook options, and build a marketing website (*right action, right time*).

While I'd always been prepared to self-publish this book, an interesting thing happened. I was contacted by a major publisher in December 2010 that got wind of the fact that I was writing this book. Not only had they already reviewed the latest version out at the time, but they were interested in publishing the book as-is.

I asked them if my model for writing and selling the book so far would be a deal breaker. On the contrary, they wished more authors wrote their books this way.

At first I was confused, but then it all made sense. The fact that I was able to sell 1,000 copies of the book on my own demonstrated *early traction*, which helped mitigate market risk for the publisher. This is not unlike how a latter-stage investor views a startup.

As with building a product, the ideal time to attract external resources is after product/market fit, which may or may not be the right action for you at that time.

In my case, I'm happy to say that additional conversations with other publishers, along with advice from Eric Ries, helped me determine that going the publisher route was the right action given my goals. I signed a contract with O'Reilly. Not only had the O'Reilly folks been early proponents of the Lean Startup movement, but they were also highly supportive of an official *Lean* series of books.

As of September 2011, I had sold just over 10,000 copies of *Running Lean* on my own and was writing a new and updated edition (the book you hold in your hands). This version was even further refined through countless interviews and workshops with entrepreneurs that spanned a wide

---

1 A reader and fellow Austin entrepreneur, Emiliano Villarreal, redid my illustrations and sent me the updated files. We started collaborating on other visuals and he now works with me at Spark59.

CHAPTER 2

spectrum of products (*build a continuous feedback loop with customers*). The goal was to synthesize my learning over the past year and broaden the audience beyond my initial prototypical early adopters of web-based entrepreneurs.

The timeline shown in Figure 2-2 summarizes the process I used to write the first edition of *Running Lean*.

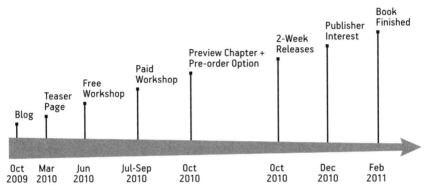

Figure 2-2. *Running Lean timeline*

Is the Book Finished?

A book, like large software, is never finished—only released.

Because I wrote this book iteratively about a topic that is still evolving, the book was just the beginning.

- I still share my raw learning on my blog.
- I write a biweekly "Running Lean Mastery" newsletter.
- Demand for my workshops has gone up.

While I love teaching these workshops, my true passion still lies in building products. Immersing myself in the world of hundreds of startups helped me identify a number of problems worth solving.

That is how Lean Canvas and USERcycle came to be.

Lean Canvas is a business model validation tool. It's a companion tool to this book that helps you document your business model, measure progress, and communicate learning with your internal and external stakeholders.

USERcycle is customer lifecycle management software that helps companies convert their users into passionate customers. Passionate customers come back and use your product, tell others about your product, and pay for your product (or get you paid).

PART 2

DOCUMENT YOUR PLAN A

Create Your Lean Canvas

Capture your business model in a portable, one-page diagram.

The Lean Canvas is the perfect format for brainstorming possible business models, prioritizing where to start, and tracking ongoing learning.

The best way to illustrate the use of the canvas is through an example. I'll describe the thought process that went into building my first product, CloudFire, using this methodology.

Brainstorm Possible Customers

When you first start out, all you have is an inkling of a problem, a solution, and maybe a customer segment. Just as rushing to build a solution can lead to waste, so can prematurely picking a customer segment or business model. The danger here is that this "selection bias" is untested and may result in a suboptimal business model or local maxima.

The Hill-Climbing Algorithm and the Problem of Local Maxima

In computer science, *hill climbing* is a mathematical optimization technique. It is an iterative algorithm that starts with an arbitrary solution to a problem, then attempts to find a better solution by incrementally changing a single element of the solution. If the change produces a better solution, an incremental change is made to the new solution, and the process is repeated until no further improvements can be found.

Hill climbing is good for finding a local optimum (a solution that cannot be improved by considering a neighboring configuration), but it is not guaranteed to find the best possible solution (the global optimum) out of all possible solutions (the search space).

Source: *http://en.wikipedia.org/wiki/Hill_climbing*

While there is no way to completely avoid the local maxima problem, you raise your odds for finding a better solution when you are initially open to exploring and even testing multiple models in parallel.

Start by brainstorming the list of possible customers for your product:

Distinguish between customers and users.

> If you have multiple user roles in your product, identify your customers.
>
> *A customer is someone who pays for your product. A user does not.*

Split broad customer segments into smaller ones.

> I've worked with startups that felt the problems they are solving are so universal, they apply to everyone.
>
> *You can't effectively build, design, and position a product for everyone.*
>
> While you might be aiming to build a mainstream product, you need to start with a specific customer in mind. Even Facebook, with its now 500 million+ users, started with a very specific user in mind: Harvard University students.

Put everyone on the same canvas at first.

> If you are building a multisided business, you might find it necessary to outline different problems, channels, and value propositions for each side of the market. I recommend starting with a single canvas first and using a different color or tag to identify each customer segment. This helps you visualize everything on a single page. Then split if needed.

Sketch a Lean Canvas for each customer segment.

As you'll find shortly, the elements of your business model can and will vary greatly by customer segment. I recommend starting with the top two or three customer segments you feel you understand the best or find most promising.

CloudFire

Background:

Prior to CloudFire, I had launched a file-sharing application called BoxCloud that simplified the process of sharing large files, using a proprietary peer-to-web (p2web) framework we had built.

BoxCloud's unique value proposition (UVP) was that it allowed the sharer to share a file/folder directly from his computer without any uploading. Recipients accessed the shared file/folder directly from their browser without the need to install any additional software.

BoxCloud was primarily targeted at business users and was in use by graphic designers, attorneys, accountants, and other small-business owners.

I was interested in exploring other uses of the p2web framework, especially around media sharing (photos, videos, and music), which is how CloudFire came about.

Really broad category:

Anyone that shares lots of media content.

More specific possible customers:

- Photographers
- Videographers
- Media consumers (scratch my own itch)
- Parents

While I was initially drawn to building something for the consumer segment (with myself as the prototypical customer), I had recently become a parent and witnessed some pain points around photo and (especially) video sharing. That is the segment I decided to model first.

Sketching a Lean Canvas

In this section, I'll outline the process for sketching a Lean Canvas.

Sketch a canvas in one sitting.

While it's tempting to iterate endlessly on the whiteboard, your initial canvas should be sketched quickly—in less than 15 minutes. The point of creating the canvas is to take a snapshot of what's in your head at this moment in time, then move on to identifying what's riskiest, and finally get out of the building and test your model with people other than yourself.

It's OK to leave sections blank.

Rather than trying to research or debate the "right" answers, put something down or leave it blank. Leaving a section blank might be indicative of what's really riskiest about your model and the place to start your testing. Some other elements, like "Unfair Advantage," take time to figure out, and your best answer right now might be "I don't know," which is also OK. The canvas is meant to be an organic document that evolves with time.

Be concise.

It's a lot easier to describe something in a paragraph than in a single sentence. The space constraints on the canvas are a great way to distill your business model down to its essence. Aim to fit your canvas on a single page.

Think in the present.

Business plans try too hard to predict the future, which is impossible. Instead, write your canvas with a "getting things done" attitude. Based on your current stage and what you know right now, what are the next sets of hypotheses you need to test to move your product forward?

Use a customer-centric approach.

Alex Osterwalder describes several techniques for approaching an initial business model canvas in his book. Since Running Lean is heavily customer-driven, I find it sufficient to start with just a customer-centric approach. As we'll see shortly, tweaking just the customer segment can completely change the business model.

When creating my canvases, I follow the prescribed order shown in Figure 3-1, which is the order the rest of the sections will follow.

PROBLEM Top 3 problems **1**	SOLUTION Top 3 features **4**	UNIQUE VALUE PROPOSITION Single, clear, compelling message that states why you are different and worth buying **3**	UNFAIR ADVANTAGE Can't be easily copied or bought **9**	CUSTOMER SEGMENTS Target customers **2**
	KEY METRICS Key activities you measure **8**		CHANNELS Path to customers **5**	
COST STRUCTURE Customer Acquisition Costs Distributing Costs Hosting People, etc. **7**			REVENUE STREAMS Revenue Model Lifetime Value Revenue Gross Margin **6**	

Lean Canvas is adapted from The Business Model Canvas (http://www.businessmodelgeneration.com) and is licensed under the Creative Commons Attribution-Share Alike 3.0 Un-ported License.

Figure 3-1. *Lean Canvas*

Problem and Customer Segments

I find that the "problem-customer segment" pair usually drives the rest of the canvas, which is why I tackle them together.

List the top one to three problems.

> For the customer segment you are working with, describe the top one to three problems they need solved. Another way to think about problems is in terms of the jobs customers need done:

> > *When people need to get a job done, they hire a product or service to do it for them. The marketer's task is to understand what jobs periodically arise in customers' lives for which they might hire products the company could make.*
> >
> > —*Clayton M. Christensen*

List existing alternatives.

> Document how you think your early adopters address these problems today. Unless you are solving a brand new problem (unlikely), most problems have existing solutions. Many times these solutions may not be from an obvious competitor.

> As an example, the biggest alternative to most online collaboration tools is not another collaboration tool, but email. Doing nothing could also be a viable alternative for a customer if the pain is not acute enough.

Identify other user roles.

Identify any other user roles that will interact with this customer. Examples:

- In a blogging platform, the customer is the blog author while the user is a reader.

- In a search engine, the customer is the advertiser while users are people running searches.

Hone in on possible early adopters.

With these problems in mind, get more specific on the customer segment. Narrow down the characteristics of your prototypical customer.

Your objective is to define an early adopter, not a mainstream customer.

CASE STUDY

CloudFire: Problem and Customer Segments

Having just become a parent, I observed the "perfect storm" of problems that I wanted to explore further, listed here and shown in Figure 3-2:

- The number of photos (and especially videos) we took increased significantly after the baby was born.
- We were sleep-deprived and found the existing solutions time-consuming and sometimes painful to use.
- The demand for this content from family (especially grandparents) and friends was high and often time-sensitive.

PROBLEM	SOLUTION	UNIQUE VALUE PROPOSITION	UNFAIR ADVANTAGE	CUSTOMER SEGMENTS
Sharing lots of photos/videos is time- consuming. Parents have no free time. There is lots of external demand on this content.				Parents (creators) Family and friends (viewers)
	KEY METRICS		CHANNELS	
Existing alternatives: Flickr Pro, SmugMug, Apple MobileMe, Facebook				*Early adopter:* Parents with young kids
COST STRUCTURE		REVENUE STREAMS		

Lean Canvas is adapted from The Business Model Canvas (http://www.businessmodelgeneration.com) and is licensed under the Creative Commons Attribution-Share Alike 3.0 Un-ported License.

Figure 3-2. *CloudFire: problem and customer segments*

Unique Value Proposition

Dead center in the Lean Canvas is a box for your UVP. This is one of the most important boxes on the canvas and also the hardest to get right.

Since writing the first version of *Running Lean*, I have refined my definition of the UVP:

> *Unique Value Proposition: Why you are different and worth ~~buying~~ getting attention.*

"Selling" is a conversation, and I believe it's too hard to do that with a single statement. More important, the first battle isn't even selling; it's getting a prospect's attention.

NOTE

First-time visitors spend eight seconds on average on a landing page. Your UVP is their first interaction with your product. Craft a good UVP and they might stay and view the rest of your site. Otherwise, they'll simply leave.

Even with this revised definition, the UVP is still hard to get right because you have to distill the essence of your product in a few words that can fit in the headline of your landing page. Additionally, your UVP also needs to be different, and that difference needs to matter.

The good news is that you don't have to get this perfect right away. Like everything on the canvas, you start with a best guess and iterate from there.

How to craft a unique value proposition

First, I highly recommend getting a copy of the classic book on marketing by Al Ries and Jack Trout: *Positioning: The Battle for Your Mind* (McGraw-Hill). Ries and Trout are considered the fathers of modern advertising. This is an "easy read" and the best crash course on marketing I've ever come across.

Here are some of my tips on how to craft a UVP:

Be different, but make sure your difference matters.

> The key to unlocking what's different about your product is deriving your UVP directly from the number-one problem you are solving. If that problem is indeed worth solving, you're more than halfway there already.

Target early adopters.

Too many marketers try to target the "middle" in the hopes of reaching mainstream customers, and in the process they water down their message. Your product is *not* ready for mainstream customers yet. Your sole job should be to find and target early adopters, which requires bold, clear, and specific messaging.

Focus on finished story benefits.

You've probably heard about the importance of highlighting benefits over features. But benefits still require your customers to translate them to their worldview. A good UVP gets inside the head of your customers and focuses on the benefits your customers derive *after* using your product.

So, for instance, if you are creating a résumé-building service:

- A feature might be "professionally designed templates."

- The benefit would be an "eye-catching résumé that stands out."

- But the finished story benefit would be "landing your dream job."

A good formula for crafting an effective UVP (by way of Dane Maxwell) is:

Instant Clarity Headline = End Result Customer Wants + Specific Period of Time + Address the Objections

---
NOTE

The second and third items in the preceding formula are great if you can use them, but they are not required.

A classic example that fits this formula is Domino's slogan:

Hot fresh pizza delivered to your door in 30 minutes or it's free.

Pick your words carefully and own them.

Words are key to any great marketing and branding campaign. Look at how the top luxury car brands have used a single word to define themselves:

- *Performance:* BMW

- *Design:* Audi

- *Prestige:* Mercedes

Picking a few "key" words that you consistently use also drives your search engine optimization (SEO) ranking.

Answer: what, who, and why.

A good UVP needs to clearly answer the first two questions—what is your product and who is your customer. The "why" is sometimes hard to fit in the same statement, and I'll frequently use a subheading for that.

Here are example UVPs I have used in products:

Lean Canvas

> *Spend More Time Building Versus Planning Your Business.*
>
> The faster, more effective way to communicate your business model

USERcycle

> *Turn your users into passionate customers.*
>
> Customer Lifecycle Management Software

Study other good UVPs.

The best way to craft a good UVP is to study the UVPs of the brands you admire. Visit their landing pages and deconstruct how and why their messaging works.

Some of my best teachers have been Apple, 37signals, and FreshBooks.

Create a high-concept pitch.

Another useful exercise is creating a high-concept pitch. High-concept pitches are used heavily by Hollywood producers to distill the general plot of a movie to a memorable sound bite. The high-concept pitch was also popularized as an effective pitching tool by Venture Hacks in its ebook, *Pitching Hacks*.

Examples:

- YouTube: "Flickr for video"

- *Aliens* (movie): "Jaws in space"

- Dogster: "Friendster for dogs"

The high-concept pitch should not be confused with a UVP and is not intended to be used on your landing page. There is a danger that the concepts the pitch is based on might be unfamiliar to your audience. For this reason, the high-concept pitch is more effective when used to quickly get your idea across and make it easy to spread, such as after a customer interview. We'll cover this specific use of the high-concept pitch in Chapter 7.

CloudFire: Unique Value Proposition

Given the current list of existing alternatives, I decided to use speed as the "difference that would matter" for my UVP and "no uploading" as the key words to position around (see Figure 3-3).

Later, you'll see how this UVP evolved significantly after just a few customer interviews.

PROBLEM	SOLUTION	UNIQUE VALUE PROPOSITION	UNFAIR ADVANTAGE	CUSTOMER SEGMENTS
Sharing lots of photos/videos is time- consuming. Parents have no free time. There is lots of external demand on this content.		The Fastest Way to Share Your Photos and Videos		Parents (creators) Family and friends (viewers)
	KEY METRICS		**CHANNELS**	
Existing alternatives: Flickr Pro, SmugMug, Apple MobileMe, Facebook		*High-level concept:* Photo and video sharing without the uploading		*Early adopter:* Parents with young kids
COST STRUCTURE			**REVENUE STREAMS**	

Lean Canvas is adapted from The Business Model Canvas (http://www.businessmodelgeneration.com) and is licensed under the Creative Commons Attribution-Share Alike 3.0 Un-ported License.

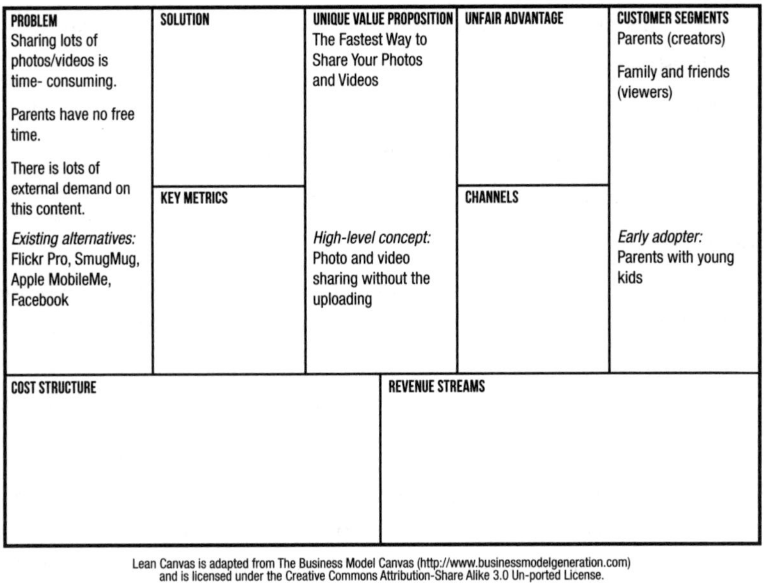

Figure 3-3. *CloudFire: UVP*

Solution

You are now ready to tackle solution possibilities.

Because all you have are untested problems, it is fairly common for them to get reprioritized or completely replaced with new ones after just a few customer interviews. For this reason, I recommend not getting carried away with fully defining your solution just yet. Rather, simply sketch out the simplest thing you could possibly build to address each problem.

Bind a solution to your problem as late as possible.

CloudFire: Solution

Based on my list of problems, I created a short list of top features I would include in the minimum viable product, or MVP (see Figure 3-4).

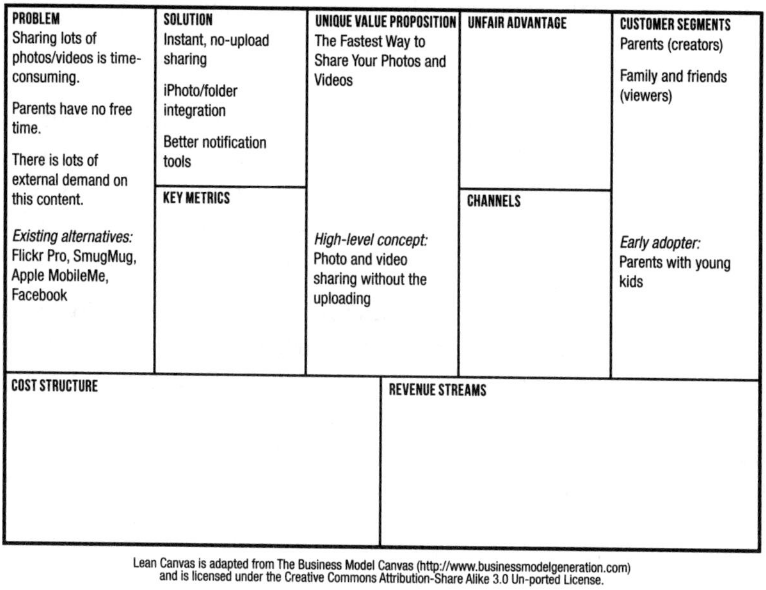

PROBLEM	SOLUTION	UNIQUE VALUE PROPOSITION	UNFAIR ADVANTAGE	CUSTOMER SEGMENTS
Sharing lots of photos/videos is time-consuming.	Instant, no-upload sharing	The Fastest Way to Share Your Photos and Videos		Parents (creators)
Parents have no free time.	iPhoto/folder integration			Family and friends (viewers)
There is lots of external demand on this content.	Better notification tools			
	KEY METRICS		**CHANNELS**	
Existing alternatives: Flickr Pro, SmugMug, Apple MobileMe, Facebook		*High-level concept:* Photo and video sharing without the uploading		*Early adopter:* Parents with young kids
COST STRUCTURE		**REVENUE STREAMS**		

Lean Canvas is adapted from The Business Model Canvas (http://www.businessmodelgeneration.com) and is licensed under the Creative Commons Attribution-Share Alike 3.0 Un-ported License.

Figure 3-4. *CloudFire: solution*

Channels

Failing to build a significant path to customers is among the top reasons why startups fail.

The initial goal of a startup is to learn, not to scale. So, at first it's OK to rely on any channels that get you in front of potential customers.

The good news is that following a "customer discovery[1]/interview" process forces you to build a path to "enough" customers early. However, if your business model relies on acquiring large numbers of customers to work, that path may not scale beyond the initial stages, and it's quite possible you'll get stuck later.

---

1   The first step described by Steve Blank in his book *The Four Steps to the Epiphany* (*http://www.cafepress.com/kandsranch*).

For this reason, it's equally important to think about your scalable channels from day one so that you may start building and testing them early.

While there are a plethora of channel options available, some channels may be outright inapplicable to your startup, while others may be more viable during later stages of your startup.

I typically look for the following characteristics in my early channels.

Freer versus paid

First, there is no such thing as a free channel. Channels we normally associate as being free, like SEO, social media, and blogging, have a nonzero human capital cost associated with them. Calculating their ROI is complicated because, unlike a paid channel that is used up after you pay for it, these channels keep working for you over time.

A commonly cited paid channel is search engine marketing (SEM). Eric Ries has written about how he tested his early product on $5 a day using Google AdWords, driving 100 clicks at a cost-per-click of 5 cents. If you can pull this off today, by all means use it, but unfortunately those days are long gone for most products. Keyword competition is so fierce now that you need to either outspend or outwit your competition. Both of these activities are better suited to the after product/market fit time frame when your focus shifts to optimizing versus learning.

Inbound versus outbound

Inbound channels use "pull messaging" to let customers find you organically, while outbound channels rely on "push messaging" to reach customers.

Examples of inbound channels:

- Blogs
- SEO
- Ebooks
- White papers
- Webinars

Examples of outbound channels:

- SEM
- Print/TV ads
- Trade shows
- Cold calling

When you don't yet have a tested value proposition, it's hard to justify spending marketing dollars or effort on outbound messaging. Getting "tech-crunched" or seeking other forms of PR before then is a form of waste. Now might be the time to start building inroads to influencers, but you are not ready to "get covered."

Interviews are a form of outbound channel that are the exception. As we'll see with the next two points, the return on learning from an interview far exceeds the cost of running an interview.

Direct versus automated

As a scalable channel, direct sales only make sense in businesses where the aggregate lifetime value of the customers exceeds the total compensation of your direct sales people, such as in certain B2B and enterprise products.

But as a learning channel, direct selling is one of the most effective, since you interact face to face with the customer.

First sell manually, then automate.

Direct versus indirect

Another area where startups waste energy is prematurely trying to establish strategic partnerships. The idea is to partner with a larger company to leverage its channels and credibility. The problem is that until you have a proven product, you won't get the right level of attention from the bigger company's sales reps to make this work. Imagine you are a sales rep at the bigger company. Given the choice of selling what you know or selling an unproven product to make your quota, which would you choose?

The same principle applies to hiring external salespeople. While a salesperson can probably outsell you on the execution of a sales plan, she can't create that plan.

You have to first sell your product yourself, before letting others do it.

Retention before referral

Many startups are obsessed with building virality and referral/affiliate programs into their product from day one. While referral programs can be very effective in spreading the word about your product, *you need to have a product worth spreading first.*

> *Build a remark-able product.*
> —*Seth Godin*, Purple Cow (*Portfolio Hardcover*)

CloudFire: Channels

I planned to start with several outbound channels (friends and other parents at daycare) for interviews, and list a few possible, more scalable channels for later (see Figure 3-5).

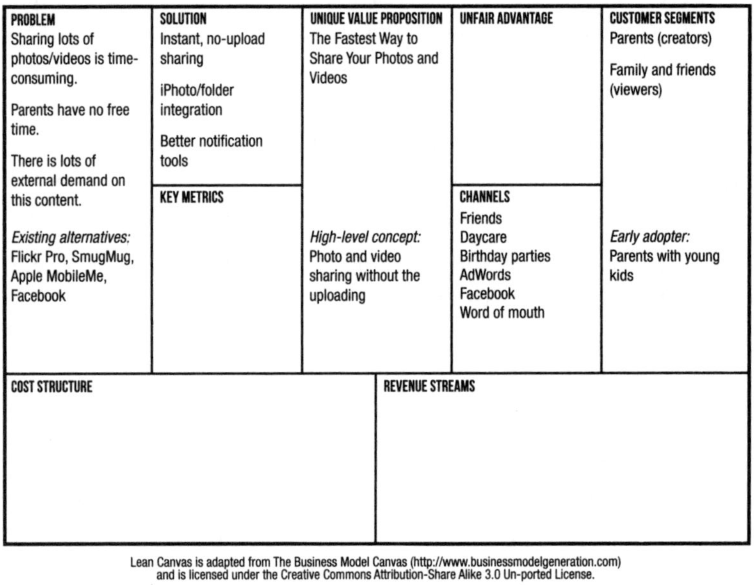

PROBLEM	SOLUTION	UNIQUE VALUE PROPOSITION	UNFAIR ADVANTAGE	CUSTOMER SEGMENTS
Sharing lots of photos/videos is time-consuming. Parents have no free time. There is lots of external demand on this content.	Instant, no-upload sharing iPhoto/folder integration Better notification tools	The Fastest Way to Share Your Photos and Videos		Parents (creators) Family and friends (viewers)
	KEY METRICS		**CHANNELS** Friends	
Existing alternatives: Flickr Pro, SmugMug, Apple MobileMe, Facebook		*High-level concept:* Photo and video sharing without the uploading	Daycare Birthday parties AdWords Facebook Word of mouth	*Early adopter:* Parents with young kids
COST STRUCTURE			**REVENUE STREAMS**	

Lean Canvas is adapted from The Business Model Canvas (http://www.businessmodelgeneration.com) and is licensed under the Creative Commons Attribution-Share Alike 3.0 Un-ported License.

Figure 3-5. CloudFire: channels

Revenue Streams and Cost Structure

The bottom two boxes, labeled "Revenue Streams" and "Cost Structure," are used to model the viability of the business. Rather than thinking in terms of three- or five-year forecasts, take a more ground-up approach.

First, model the runway you will need to define, build, and launch your MVP. Then, revise after you get there.

Revenue streams

A lot of startups choose to defer the "pricing question" because they don't think their product is ready. Something I hear a lot is that an MVP is, by definition, embarrassingly minimal. How can you possibly charge for it?

First, an MVP is not synonymous with a half-baked or buggy product. Your MVP should address not only the *top problems* customers have identified as being important to them, but also the problems that are *worth solving*. By that definition, you should plan to deliver enough value to justify charging.

But there is another line of reasoning that is frequently cited for deferring pricing: to accelerate initial learning. The argument goes that pricing creates unnecessary friction that should be avoided early on.

The mindset most of us have when we're launching a new product is one of *lowering signup friction*. We want to make it as easy as possible for the customer to say yes and agree to take a chance on our product, hoping the value we deliver over time will earn us the privilege of his business.

Not only does this approach delay validation of one of the riskier parts of the model (because it's too easy for a user to say yes), but a lack of strong customer "commitment" can also be detrimental to optimal learning.

Furthermore, you don't need a lot of users to support learning—*just a few good customers.*

I believe that if you intend to charge for your product, you should charge from day one.

NOTE

A reasonable exception is when you're offering a value proposition that is built over time—for example, premium LinkedIn accounts.

Here's why:

Price is part of the product.

Suppose I place two bottles of water in front of you and tell you that one costs 50 cents and the other costs 2 dollars. Despite the fact that you wouldn't be able to tell them apart in a blind taste test (the products are similar enough), you might be inclined to believe (or at least wonder) whether the more expensive water is of higher quality.

Here, price has the power to change your perception of the product.

Price defines your customers.

More interesting is the fact that the bottled water you pick determines your customer segment. From the existing market for bottled water, we know there is a viable business for bottled water at both price segments. What you charge signals your positioning on which customers you want to attract.

Getting paid is the first form of validation.

Getting a customer to give you money is one of the hardest actions you can ask them to take and is an early form of product validation.

Although there is a lot of science around pricing, pricing is more art than science. For a great primer, I highly recommend getting a copy of Neil Davidson's free ebook on software pricing, *Don't Just Roll the Dice.*

One technique for setting initial pricing is pricing against the list of existing alternatives from the Problem box. These alternatives provide reference price anchors against which your offering will be measured.

(For more specific techniques for pricing Software as a Service [SaaS] products, including when to use freemium pricing, see "How to Set Pricing for a SaaS Product" in the Appendix.)

Cost structure

List the operational costs you will incur while taking your product to market. It's hard to accurately calculate these too far into the future. Instead, focus on the present:

- What will it cost you to interview 30 to 50 customers?

- What will it cost you to build and launch your MVP?

- What will your ongoing burn rate look like in terms of both fixed and variable costs?

Use the revenue streams and cost structure inputs to calculate a break-even point and estimate how much time, money, and effort you need to get there. You will use this later to prioritize which model you start with.

CloudFire: Revenue Streams and Cost Structure

Using the existing alternatives for price anchoring, which ranged from $24 to $39 per year for Flickr and SmugMug, to $99/year for Apple's MobileMe (a lot more than just photos/videos), I decided to start with $49/year pricing.

Prints (and other merchandise) were also revenue streams these companies used, but I wasn't sure if enough people still purchased prints anymore to make it worthwhile (a hypothesis that would need to be tested). More important, prints represented a potential secondary revenue stream that could only be realized once customers derived a core UVP. For this reason, I left out prints from both the MVP and initial canvas (see Figure 3-6).

The only initial costs to getting an MVP out were people costs, which I list in the next section.

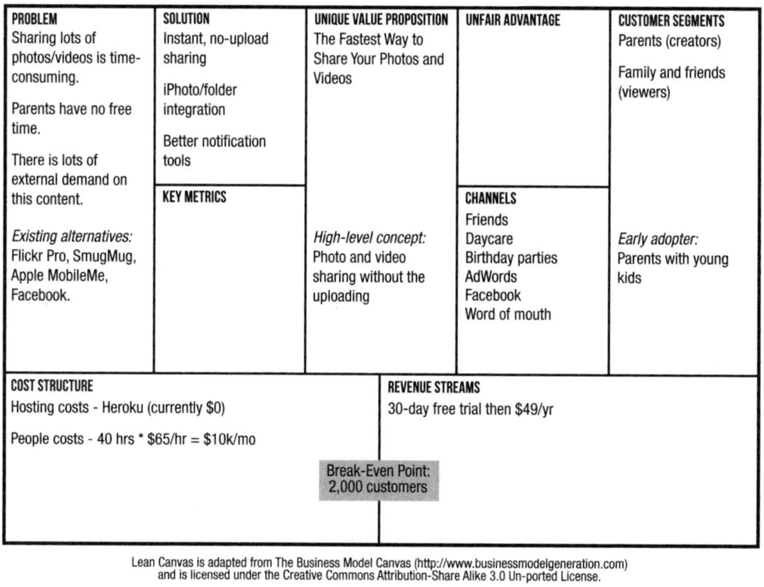

PROBLEM	SOLUTION	UNIQUE VALUE PROPOSITION	UNFAIR ADVANTAGE	CUSTOMER SEGMENTS
Sharing lots of photos/videos is time-consuming. Parents have no free time. There is lots of external demand on this content. *Existing alternatives:* Flickr Pro, SmugMug, Apple MobileMe, Facebook.	Instant, no-upload sharing iPhoto/folder integration Better notification tools **KEY METRICS**	The Fastest Way to Share Your Photos and Videos *High-level concept:* Photo and video sharing without the uploading	**CHANNELS** Friends Daycare Birthday parties AdWords Facebook Word of mouth	Parents (creators) Family and friends (viewers) *Early adopter:* Parents with young kids

COST STRUCTURE	REVENUE STREAMS
Hosting costs - Heroku (currently $0) People costs - 40 hrs * $65/hr = $10k/mo	30-day free trial then $49/yr

Break-Even Point:
2,000 customers

Lean Canvas is adapted from The Business Model Canvas (http://www.businessmodelgeneration.com) and is licensed under the Creative Commons Attribution-Share Alike 3.0 Un-ported License.

Figure 3-6. CloudFire: revenue streams and cost structure

Key Metrics

Find the key number that tells you how your business is doing in real time, before you get the sales report.

—Norm Brodsky and Bo Burlingham,
The Knack (Portfolio Hardcover)

Every business has a few key numbers that can be used to measure how well it is performing. These numbers are key for both measuring progress and identifying hot spots in your customer lifecycle.

A model I use heavily is Dave McClure's Pirate Metrics,[2] shown in Figure 3-7.

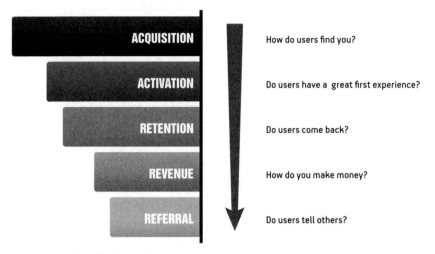

Figure 3-7. *CloudFire: Pirate Metrics*

Even though Pirate Metrics was built with software companies in mind, the model is applicable to many different types of businesses. Let's walk through each step using a flower shop and a software product as examples.

Acquisition

Acquisition describes the point when you turn an unaware visitor into an interested prospect.

In the case of the flower shop, getting someone walking by your window to stop and come in to your shop is an acquisition event.

On a product website, getting someone to do anything other than leave your website (abandon) is a measure of acquisition. I specifically measure successful acquisition as getting my visitors to view my signup page.

Activation

Activation describes the point when the interested customer has his first gratifying user experience.

---

2 Dave McClure called them Pirate Metrics because when you put the first letter in each funnel step together, they spell the word: AARRR.

In the case of the flower shop, if the prospect found the shop in disarray once he comes inside, there would be a disconnect with the promise made at the front of the store. That wouldn't be a gratifying first user experience.

On the product site, once the prospect signs up, you have to make sure you get the customer to a point where he can connect the promise you made on your landing page (your UVP) with your product.

Retention

Retention measures "repeated use" and/or engagement with your product.

So, in the case of the flower shop, the action of coming back to the store—and in the case of the product website, the act of logging back in to use the product again—would count toward retention.

As we'll see in Part 4 of the book, this is one of the key metrics to measuring product/market fit.

Revenue

Revenue measures the events that get you paid.

These could be buying flowers or buying a subscription for your product. These events may or may not occur on the first visit.

Referral

Referral is a more advanced form of a user acquisition channel where your happy customers refer or drive potential prospects into your conversion funnel.

In the case of the flower shop, this could be as simple as telling another friend about the store.

For the software product, this could range from implicit viral or social sharing features (like Share with a friend), to explicit affiliate referral programs or Net Promoter Score.

CloudFire: Key Metrics

In Figure 3-8 I map specific user actions that correspond to each of the key metrics discussed earlier.

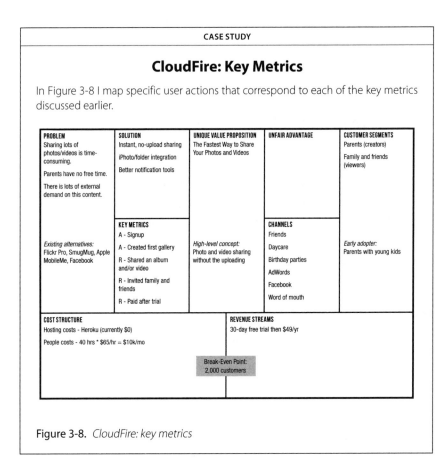

PROBLEM	SOLUTION	UNIQUE VALUE PROPOSITION	UNFAIR ADVANTAGE	CUSTOMER SEGMENTS
Sharing lots of photos/videos is time-consuming. Parents have no free time. There is lots of external demand on this content.	Instant, no-upload sharing iPhoto/folder integration Better notification tools	The Fastest Way to Share Your Photos and Videos		Parents (creators) Family and friends (viewers)
Existing alternatives: Flickr Pro, SmugMug, Apple MobileMe, Facebook	**KEY METRICS** A - Signup A - Created first gallery R - Shared an album and/or video R - Invited family and friends R - Paid after trial	*High-level concept:* Photo and video sharing without the uploading	**CHANNELS** Friends Daycare Birthday parties AdWords Facebook Word of mouth	*Early adopter:* Parents with young kids

COST STRUCTURE	REVENUE STREAMS
Hosting costs - Heroku (currently $0) People costs - 40 hrs * $65/hr = $10k/mo	30-day free trial then $49/yr

Break-Even Point:
2,000 customers

Figure 3-8. *CloudFire: key metrics*

Unfair Advantage

This is usually the hardest section to fill, which is why I leave it for last. Most founders list things as competitive advantages that really aren't— such as passion, lines of code, or features.

Another frequently cited advantage in business models is the "first-mover" advantage. However, it doesn't take much to see that being first can actually be a disadvantage, as most of the hard work of paving new ground (risk mitigation) falls on your shoulders, only to be potentially picked up later by fast-followers unless you're able to constantly outpace them with a real "unfair advantage." None of these companies were first movers: Ford, Toyota, Google, Microsoft, Apple, or Facebook.

An interesting perspective (via Jason Cohen) to keep in mind is that anything worth copying will be copied, especially once you start to demonstrate a viable business model.

Imagine a scenario where your cofounder steals your source code, sets up shop in Costa Rica, and slashes prices. Do you still have a business? How about if Google or Apple launches a competitive product and drops the price to $0?

You have to be able to build a successful business in spite of that, which led Jason Cohen to offer the following definition:[3]

> *A real unfair advantage is something that cannot be easily copied or bought.*
>
> —*Jason Cohen*, A Smart Bear *blog*

Here are some examples of real unfair advantages that fit this definition:

- Insider information
- The right "expert" endorsements
- A dream team
- Personal authority
- Large network effects
- Community
- Existing customers
- SEO ranking

Some unfair advantages can also start out as values that become differentiators over time.

For example, Zappos CEO Tony Hsieh believes strongly in creating happiness for his customers and employees. This manifested itself in many company policies that, on the surface, didn't make much business sense, such as allowing customer service representatives to spend as much time as was needed to make a customer happy and offering a 365-day return policy with two-way paid shipping. But these policies served to differentiate the Zappos brand and build a large, passionate, and vocal customer base that played a large role in the company's eventual $1.2 billion acquisition by Amazon in 2009.

You may have to leave this box blank when you first start out, but it's here to make you really think about how you can/will make yourself different and make your difference matter.

---

3 Jason Cohen. "No, that IS NOT a competitive advantage"; *http://blog.asmartbear.com/ not-competitive-advantage.html*.

CloudFire: Unfair Advantage

Even though CloudFire is built on a proprietary p2web framework that might give us an early advantage, anything worth copying will be copied. So I decide to base my unfair advantage on something harder to replicate. In this case, community (see Figure 3-9).

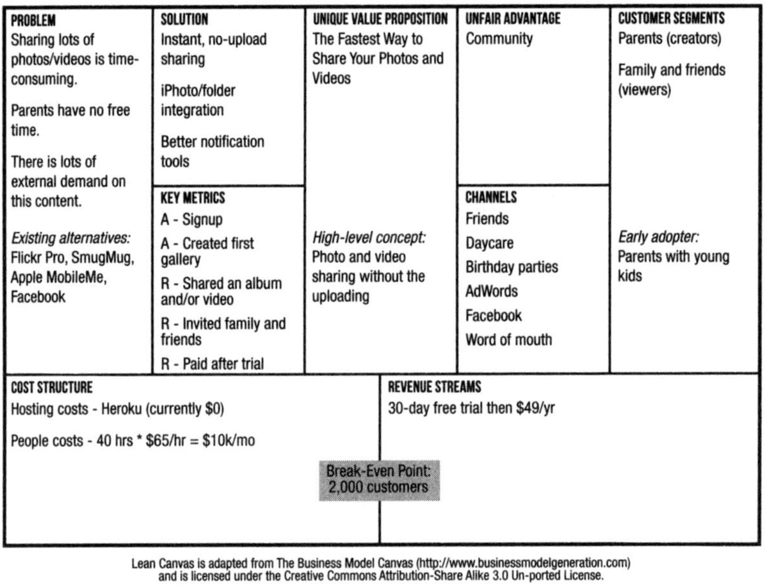

PROBLEM	SOLUTION	UNIQUE VALUE PROPOSITION	UNFAIR ADVANTAGE	CUSTOMER SEGMENTS
Sharing lots of photos/videos is time-consuming.	Instant, no-upload sharing	The Fastest Way to Share Your Photos and Videos	Community	Parents (creators)
Parents have no free time.	iPhoto/folder integration			Family and friends (viewers)
There is lots of external demand on this content.	Better notification tools			
	KEY METRICS		**CHANNELS**	
	A - Signup		Friends	
Existing alternatives:	A - Created first gallery	*High-level concept:* Photo and video sharing without the uploading	Daycare	*Early adopter:* Parents with young kids
Flickr Pro, SmugMug, Apple MobileMe, Facebook	R - Shared an album and/or video		Birthday parties AdWords	
	R - Invited family and friends		Facebook	
	R - Paid after trial		Word of mouth	

COST STRUCTURE	REVENUE STREAMS
Hosting costs - Heroku (currently $0)	30-day free trial then $49/yr
People costs - 40 hrs * $65/hr = $10k/mo	

Break-Even Point:
2,000 customers

Lean Canvas is adapted from The Business Model Canvas (http://www.businessmodelgeneration.com) and is licensed under the Creative Commons Attribution-Share Alike 3.0 Un-ported License.

Figure 3-9. *CloudFire: unfair advantage*

Now It's Your Turn

Documenting your Plan A is a prerequisite for moving on. Too many founders carry their hypotheses in their heads alone, which makes it hard to systematically build and test a business.

You have to draw a line in the sand.

How you create your Lean Canvas is up to you.

You can:

- Visit *http://LeanCanvas.com* and create your online canvas there.

- Create a version in PowerPoint or Keynote.

- Sketch a canvas on paper.

The important thing is to share your Lean Canvas with at least one other person when you are done.

PART 3

IDENTIFY THE RISKIEST PARTS OF YOUR PLAN

CHAPTER 4

Prioritize Where to Start

Now that you have a list of possible models, the next step is to prioritize where to start. Otherwise, it's easy to fall into the trap of making marginal progress, only to get stuck later.

Incorrect prioritization of risk is one of the top contributors of waste.

What Is Risk?

Before moving on, it helps to define what I mean by risk. We know that startups are highly uncertain, but uncertainty and risk aren't the same thing. We can be uncertain about a lot of things that aren't risky.

Douglas Hubbard makes a clear distinction between the two in his book, *How to Measure Anything* (Wiley):

> *Uncertainty: The lack of complete certainty, that is, the existence of more than one possibility.*

> *Risk: A state of uncertainty where some of the possibilities involve a loss, catastrophe, or other undesirable outcome.*

The good news is that the Lean Canvas automatically captures uncertainties that also are risks—the loss here can be quantified both in terms of opportunity costs and real costs. But not all these risks are equal.

The way you quantify risk in your business model is by quantifying the probabilities of a specific outcome along with quantifying the associated loss if you're wrong. This is a key step to prioritizing what's riskiest on your business model and determining where to start.

For instance, in the "How I Iterated This Book" case study from Chapter 2, I didn't consider pricing for the book as high risk. The reason for this is that even though the loss of nobody buying the book would be huge, the probability of that happening was low provided I wrote a "good" book. That is why I shifted my focus early to testing the "Table of Contents" versus the price.

Risks in a startup can be divided into three general categories, listed here and depicted in Figure 4-1:

Product risk

> Getting the product right

Customer risk

> Building a path to customers

Market risk

> Building a viable business

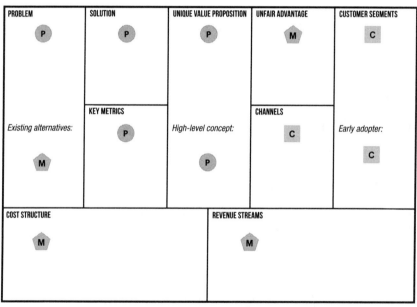

Lean Canvas is adapted from The Business Model Canvas (http://www.businessmodelgeneration.com) and is licensed under the Creative Commons Attribution-Share Alike 3.0 Un-ported License.

Figure 4-1. *Risks*

Tackling all these risks at once can be overwhelming, which is why you need to prioritize them based on the stage of your product, and tackle them systematically.

There is a whole science to quantifying and measuring risks using probabilities and statistical modeling techniques. If you are so inclined, get a copy of Douglas Hubbard's book, which is a great read even for qualitative measurements like customer interviewing results.

I am not recommending using a statistical model to measure risks on your Lean Canvas, but even a basic understanding of how to ballpark relative risks on your canvas goes a long way toward prioritizing where to start. While what is riskiest in your model will vary depending on the type of product you're building, I've found some initial risks to be universal and a good starting point for ranking business models, which we'll cover next.

Rank Your Business Models

It's time to lay your Lean Canvases side by side and prioritize which models to start with.

Your objective is to find a model with a *big enough market* you can *reach* with customers who *need your product* that *you can build a business* around.

Here is the weighting order I use (from highest to lowest):

1. *Customer pain level (Problem)*

   Prioritize customer segments that you believe will need your product the most. The goal is to have one or more of your top three problems as must-haves for them.

2. *Ease of reach (Channels)*

   Building a path to customers is one of the harder aspects of building a successful product. If you have an easier path to one segment of customers over others, take that into consideration. It doesn't guarantee you'll find a problem worth solving or a viable business model, but it will get you out of the building faster and speed up your learning.

3. *Price/gross margin (Revenue Streams/Cost Structure)*

   What you can charge for your product is largely driven by the customer segment. Pick a customer segment that allows you to maximize on your margins. The more money you get to keep, the fewer customers you need to reach to break even.

4. *Market size (Customer Segments)*

   Pick a customer segment that represents a big enough market given the goals for your business.

5. *Technical feasibility (Solution)*

   Visit your Solution box to ensure that your planned solution not only is feasible, but also represents the minimum feature set to put in front of customers.

CloudFire: Prioritize Where to Start

Figures 4-2 through 4-5 depict all the CloudFire Lean Canvases followed by their ranking.

PROBLEM	SOLUTION	UNIQUE VALUE PROPOSITION	UNFAIR ADVANTAGE	CUSTOMER SEGMENTS
Sharing lots of photos/videos is time-consuming.	Instant, no-upload sharing	The Fastest Way to Share Your Photos and Videos	Community	Parents (creators)
Parents have no free time.	iPhoto/folder integration			Family and friends (viewers)
There is lots of external demand on this content.	Better notification tools			
	KEY METRICS		**CHANNELS**	
	A - Sign-up		Friends	
Existing alternatives: Flickr Pro, SmugMug, Apple MobileMe, Facebook	A - Created first gallery	*High-level concept:* Photo and video sharing without the uploading	Daycare	*Early adopter:* Parents with young kids
	R - Shared an album and/or video		Birthday parties	
			AdWords	
	R - Invited family and friends		Facebook	
	R - Paid after trial		Word of mouth	

COST STRUCTURE	REVENUE STREAMS
Hosting costs - Heroku (currently $0)	30-day free trial then $49/yr
People costs - 40 hrs * $65/hr = $10k/mo	

Break-Even Point: 2,000 customers

Lean Canvas is adapted from The Business Model Canvas (http://www.businessmodelgeneration.com) and is licensed under the Creative Commons Attribution-Share Alike 3.0 Un-ported License.

Figure 4-2. CloudFire: Parents Lean Canvas

PROBLEM	SOLUTION	UNIQUE VALUE PROPOSITION	UNFAIR ADVANTAGE	CUSTOMER SEGMENTS
Sharing lots of photos/videos is time-consuming.	Instant, no-upload sharing	The Fastest Way to Share Your Photos and Videos	Community	Photographers (creators)
Most proofing sites only support low-res thumbnails.	Aperture/Lightroom/folder integration			Clients (viewers)
	Cloud storage of originals			
	KEY METRICS		**CHANNELS**	
	Created first gallery		First-degree network	
Existing alternatives: SmugMug Pro, Photo Shelter	Shared an album and/or video	*High-level concept:* Photo and video sharing without the uploading	Cold calling	*Early adopter:* Wedding photographers, sports photographers, portrait photographers
	Invited clients		Photography events	

COST STRUCTURE	REVENUE STREAMS
Hosting costs - Heroku (currently $0)	30-day free trial then $199/yr
People costs - 40 hrs * $65/hr = $10k/mo	

Break-Even Point: 600 customers

Lean Canvas is adapted from The Business Model Canvas (http://www.businessmodelgeneration.com) and is licensed under the Creative Commons Attribution-Share Alike 3.0 Un-ported License.

Figure 4-3. CloudFire: Photographers Lean Canvas

—continued—

PROBLEM	SOLUTION	UNIQUE VALUE PROPOSITION	UNFAIR ADVANTAGE	CUSTOMER SEGMENTS
Sharing large video files is time-consuming and error prone. Most proofing sites only support low-res thumbnails. *Existing alternatives:* FTP, CDN	Instant no-upload sharing Progressive streaming **KEY METRICS** Create first project Shared video Invited clients	The Fastest Way to Share Your Video Files *High-level concept:* Video sharing without uploading	??? **CHANNELS** First-degree network Cold calling	Videographers (creators) Clients (viewers) *Early adopter:* Music, sports, video games

COST STRUCTURE	REVENUE STREAMS
Hosting costs - Heroku (currently $0) People costs - 40 hrs * $65/hr = $10k/mo	30-day free trial then $99/mo **Break-Even Point:** **100 customers**

Lean Canvas is adapted from The Business Model Canvas (http://www.businessmodelgeneration.com) and is licensed under the Creative Commons Attribution-Share Alike 3.0 Un-ported License.

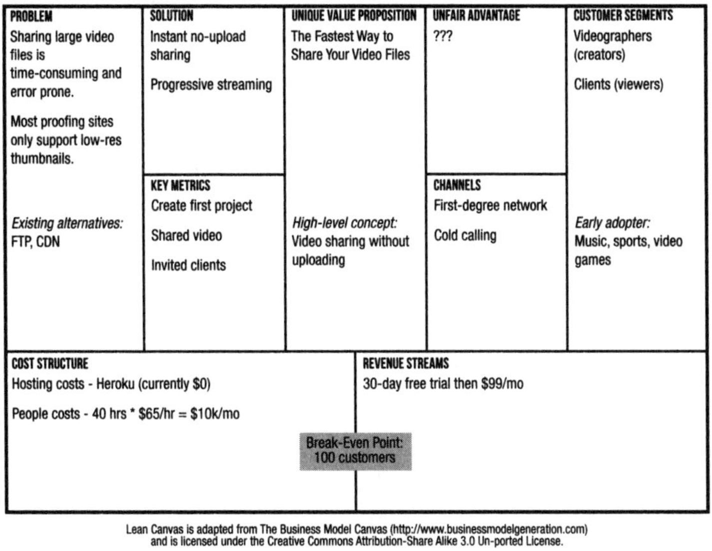

Figure 4-4. *CloudFire: Videographers Lean Canvas*

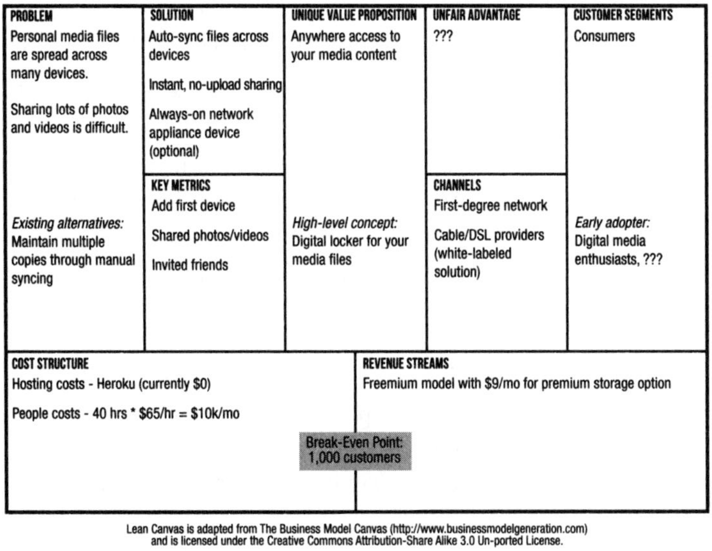

PROBLEM	SOLUTION	UNIQUE VALUE PROPOSITION	UNFAIR ADVANTAGE	CUSTOMER SEGMENTS
Personal media files are spread across many devices. Sharing lots of photos and videos is difficult. *Existing alternatives:* Maintain multiple copies through manual syncing	Auto-sync files across devices Instant, no-upload sharing Always-on network appliance device (optional) **KEY METRICS** Add first device Shared photos/videos Invited friends	Anywhere access to your media content *High-level concept:* Digital locker for your media files	??? **CHANNELS** First-degree network Cable/DSL providers (white-labeled solution)	Consumers *Early adopter:* Digital media enthusiasts, ???

COST STRUCTURE	REVENUE STREAMS
Hosting costs - Heroku (currently $0) People costs - 40 hrs * $65/hr = $10k/mo	Freemium model with $9/mo for premium storage option **Break-Even Point:** **1,000 customers**

Lean Canvas is adapted from The Business Model Canvas (http://www.businessmodelgeneration.com) and is licensed under the Creative Commons Attribution-Share Alike 3.0 Un-ported License.

Figure 4-5. *CloudFire: Consumers Lean Canvas*

Even though the Videographers customer segment had the highest potential margins, it also represented the model that would be technically most challenging because our existing technology hadn't been proven to work with really large files (large size is typical of video files). The Consumer segment represented the weakest value proposition and was a hard monetization model to pull off. Based on these rankings, I decide to prioritize starting with the Parents and Photographers customer segments.

Seek External Advice

Another effective technique for further calibrating your risks is getting out of the building and validating them with people other than yourself.[1]

It is imperative that you share your model with at least one other person.

I used to advocate jumping right into customer interviews after documenting my initial models, but now I prefer to first spend a little additional time prioritizing risks and brainstorming alternative models with people other than customers—e.g., advisors.

The main reason I do this is to maximize speed and learning. Customers cannot directly give you all the answers, and due to the iterative and qualitative nature of early learning, validating hypotheses takes time. Furthermore, you might still be targeting too broad a customer segment, too small a customer segment, or the wrong customer segment altogether.

The "right" advisors, on the other hand, can help you identify risks on the "total plan" and help you to further refine and/or outright eliminate some models.

I use the term *advisor* rather loosely. An early advisor might be a prototypical customer, a potential investor, or another entrepreneur with specific expertise, domain knowledge, or experiential knowledge that applies to you.

For instance, since selling my last company, I've shared my lessons learned on CloudFire with several other entrepreneurs who were also looking to target the Parents customer segment. I estimate that my advice and specific tactics have saved them somewhere in the ballpark of three to four months, which is hugely valuable, especially in the earliest stages.

Here are some guidelines for running business model interviews:

Avoid the 10-slide deck.

> I completely avoid a traditional "10-slide deck" because the point of the interview is learning versus pitching. The other extreme, no slides, although most natural, requires practice and may not lead to as many actionable insights because it may be hard for the other person to retain everything you tell her.

> My tool of choice is an incremental build of the Lean Canvas delivered on an iPad (or paper). I start with a blank canvas and incrementally reveal parts of the business model as I walk through it.

---

1   This is a technique that Douglas Hubbard describes as the "Instinctive Bayesian Approach" in his book.

Devote 20% of your time to setup, 80% to conversation.

The stacked flow allows me to pace the conversation and leave all the information on the screen. It usually takes me three to five minutes to walk through my model; then I shut up and listen.

I have found that leaving the complete canvas open in front of people always evokes a reaction because people can visualize the entire model and they always have an opinion.

Ask specific questions.

I specifically want to know:

- What do they consider to be the riskiest aspect of this plan?

- Have they overcome similar risks? How?

- How would they go about testing these risks?

- Are there other people I should speak with?

Be wary of the "advisor paradox."

As we'll see shortly, just as customer interviews aren't about asking customers what they want, these interviews aren't about asking advisors what to do.

The Advisor Paradox: Hire advisors for good advice but don't follow it, apply it.

—Venture Hacks

The key is not to take this feedback as either "judgment" or "validation," but rather as a means of *identifying and prioritizing risk*.

It is still your job to *own* your business model. But because you don't have all the answers, you need to build your startup through a series of conversations—with advisors, customers, investors, and even competitors.

Success is unlocked at the intersection of these conversations, and it's your job as the entrepreneur to synthesize it into a coherent whole.

Recruit visionary advisors.

Much like early adopters want to help when you nail their problems, visionary advisors will want to help when you present them with interesting problems that trigger their strengths and passion.

You'll know if there's a fit based on their answers and body language. If so, consider bringing them on as formal advisors.

CHAPTER 5

Get Ready to Experiment

With your starting models and risks prioritized, now you need to get ready to run experiments.

Assemble a Problem/Solution Team

Before you start running your first set of experiments, it's important to assemble the right team.

Forget Traditional Departments

In a Lean Startup, traditional department labels like "Engineering," "QA," "Marketing," and so forth can get in the way and create needless friction. Eric Ries instead recommends organizing around two teams, the Problem team and the Solution team.

The Problem team

> The Problem team is *mostly* involved with "outside-the-building" activities such as interviewing customers, running usability tests, and so on.

The Solution team

> The Solution team is *mostly* involved with "inside-the-building" activities such as writing code, running tests, deploying releases, and so on.

I say "mostly" because these teams need to be highly cross-functional with overlapping members. Also, interacting with customers is everyone's responsibility.

While I agree with the logical distinction between Problem and Solution teams, at this stage of a product, you're best served with having a single Problem/Solution team.

Start with the Smallest Team Possible, but No Smaller

The ideal Problem/Solution team size is two or three people.

There are many arguments for building your Release 1.0 (minimum viable product, or MVP) with a small team:

- Communication is easier.

- You build less.

- You keep costs low.

I built CloudFire "mostly" as a single founder. The biggest challenge I faced was balancing outside-the-building activities with inside-the-building activities, and I had to come up with a set of work hacks to make this work (see "How to Achieve Flow in a Lean Startup" in the Appendix).

While it is possible to build a product by yourself, I highly recommend working with at least one other person who can, at a minimum, help to enforce periodic reality checks. Ideally, this is a cofounder, but advisors, investors, and even an ad hoc board made up of other startup founders can fill this role.

More important than the number of members is ensuring that you have the right talents within the team to iterate quickly.

The three must-haves: development, design, and marketing

You don't always need three people to complete the team. Sometimes you can find these talents across two people, and other times all you need is one person. I tend to look for people with some level of expertise in all three areas.

Here's how I define them:

Development

> If you are building a product, you need strong product development skills on your team. Having prior experience building stuff is key, along with expertise in the specific technology you are using.

Design

By "design" I mean both aesthetics and usability. In newer markets, function can take precedence over form, but we live in an increasingly "design-aware" world where form cannot be ignored. Also, a product is not just a collection of features but rather a collection of user flows. You need people on your team that can deliver on the right experience that matches your customers' worldview.

Marketing

Everything else is marketing. Marketing drives the external perception of your product, and you need people that can put themselves in the shoes of your customer. Good copywriting and communication skills are key here, along with an understanding of metrics, pricing, and positioning.

Be Wary of Outsourcing Your Problem/Solution Team

I constantly run across teams that try to outsource one or more of these three areas, which is usually a bad idea. While you might be able to outsource an early prototype or demo, be wary of putting yourself at the mercy of someone else's schedule, as that can limit your ability to both iterate quickly and learn.

The one thing you should *never* outsource is learning about customers.

Running Effective Experiments

In this section, I'll lay a few ground rules for defining and running effective experiments.

Maximize for Speed, Learning, and Focus

Because the goal of a startup is to find a plan that works before running out of resources, we know that *speed*, as measured by cycle time around the Build-Measure-Learn loop shown in Figure 5-1, is important. We also know that learning—specifically, *learning about customers*—is important. But something that doesn't get nearly enough attention is *focus*.

You need all three—speed, learning, and focus—to run an optimal experiment. Let's see what happens when you don't have all three (see Figure 5-2).

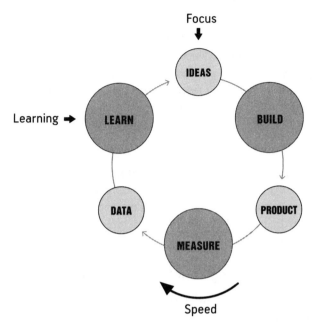

Figure 5-1. *Speed, learning, and focus*

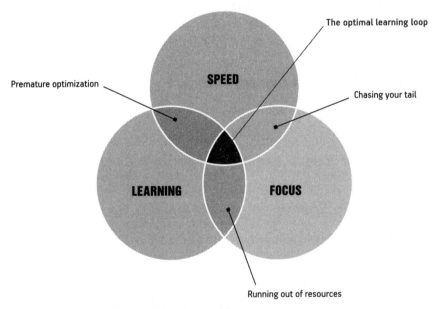

Figure 5-2. *Maximize for speed, learning, and focus*

Speed and focus

When you are going fast and are focused but not learning, the image of a dog chasing its tail comes to mind. You are expending a lot of energy but simply going around in circles.

Learning and focus

When you are focused on the right thing and learning but you are not moving quickly enough, you stand the danger of running out of resources or getting outpaced by a competitor.

Speed and learning

Finally, when you are going fast and learning but you are not focused, you can fall into the premature optimization trap. Some examples of premature optimization are scaling servers when you have no customers, and optimizing landing pages when you don't yet have a product that works.

Identify a Single Key Metric or Goal

A startup can focus on only one metric. So you have to decide what that is and ignore everything else.

—Noah Kagan

When formulating an experiment, stay focused on the key learning or key metric you need to achieve, which will vary by the type and stage of your product. While it's possible to tackle multiple metrics and goals simultaneously, I've always found it most effective to stay singularly focused.

Do the Smallest Thing Possible to Learn

The best is often the enemy of the good.

—Voltaire

Challenge yourself to find the simplest thing you can do to test a hypothesis. This is an underappreciated skill. Once you truly understand what's riskiest about your product, it's often possible to build something other than the product to test it.

You don't need code to test a software product. (Dropbox)

While building Dropbox at MIT, Drew Houston posted a three-minute demo on Hacker News that went viral. The video-plus-teaser landing page helped him attract tens of thousands of early adopters, find a cofounder, and get accepted into Y Combinator. At the time, Drew estimated his launch date at less than three months away. It took him 18 months to publicly launch Dropbox.

Formulate a Falsifiable Hypothesis

What most people write down for their business model is really not yet in a form that is testable. The Lean Startup methodology is heavily rooted in the scientific method and requires that you convert these assumptions into falsifiable hypotheses.

A falsifiable hypothesis is a statement that can be clearly proven wrong.

When you skip this step, you can easily fall into the trap of accumulating just enough evidence to convince yourself that your hypothesis is correct.

This is best illustrated with an example.

Here are two statements that describe a channel hypothesis:

Too vague

Being known as an "expert" will drive early adopters.

Specific and testable

A blog post will drive 100 signups.

The first statement is a hypothesis that cannot be proven wrong because the expected outcome of driving early adopters is not measurable. Specifically, it is not clear how many early adopters are needed to prove this hypothesis to be true—1 or 100 or 1,000—or what "being an expert" really entails.

The second statement not only has a specific and measurable outcome, but it is also based on a specific and repeatable action that makes it testable. Even if you fail to hit the expected outcome, the mere action of declaring it up front is hugely valuable, not only for enforcing a reality check, but also for improving your judgment.

A formula for crafting a falsifiable hypothesis is:

Falsifiable Hypothesis = [Specific Repeatable Action] will [Expected Measurable Outcome]

Validate Qualitatively, Verify Quantitatively

Before product/market fit, the terrain is riddled with extreme uncertainty. The good news is when you have a lot of uncertainty, you don't need a lot of data to learn.

If you have a lot of uncertainty now, you don't need much data to reduce uncertainty significantly. When you have a lot of certainty already, then you need a lot of data to reduce uncertainty significantly.

—*Douglas Hubbard*

This naturally works to your advantage.

Your initial goal is to get a strong signal (positive or negative) that typically doesn't require a large sample size. You might be able to do this with *as few as five customer interviews*.[1]

A strong negative signal indicates that your bold hypothesis most likely won't work and lets you quickly refine or abandon it. However, a strong positive signal doesn't necessarily mean your hypothesis will scale up to statistical significance; nevertheless, it gives you permission to move forward on the hypothesis until it can be verified later through quantitative data.

---

1 This number comes from usability-testing research (via Jakob Nielsen/Steve Krug) that shows how five testers are enough to uncover 85% of the problems. We'll also see some specific examples later in the book where I've been able to verify this claim.

Validating hypotheses in this way—*first qualitatively, then quantitatively*—is a key principle we'll see applied in various stages throughout this book.

Make Sure You Can Correlate Results Back to Specific Actions

One of the harder things to do is to correlate measured results back to specific and repeatable actions, as your product is always changing. When running qualitative experiments (like interviews), it's important to run them the same way until certain repeatable patterns emerge. For quantitative experiments, techniques like cohort analysis and split testing allow you to achieve this. We'll cover this in more detail a bit later.

Create Accessible Dashboards

Testing hypotheses can be scary for founders. This is understandable, as startup founders pour their blood, sweat, and tears into their work. They have a lot riding on the outcome of their efforts and don't like to be proven wrong.

But without a level of transparency and objectivity, there is a danger of running your startup primarily on faith. It is imperative to openly share your experiments company-wide.

> *A business should be run like an aquarium, where everybody can see what's going on.*
>
> —*Jack Stack,* The Great Game of Business *(Currency/Doubleday)*

Communicate Learning Early and Often

Company-wide dashboards are great for on-the-ground tactical analysis, but it is equally important to report on your learning milestones at a strategic level.

A good way to do this is to periodically communicate the lessons learned from your last batch of experiments—weekly with your internal team and at least monthly with your external advisors and investors. This lets you pause, reflect on your findings as a team, and better plan the next set of activities (i.e., hypotheses to test).

The last two steps form the basis of what Eric Ries describes as "Innovation Accounting" in his book *The Lean Startup* (Crown Business). Figure 5-3 shows my implementation of an Innovation Accounting model I use, which combines ongoing learning with Lean Canvas and a cohort-based conversion dashboard.

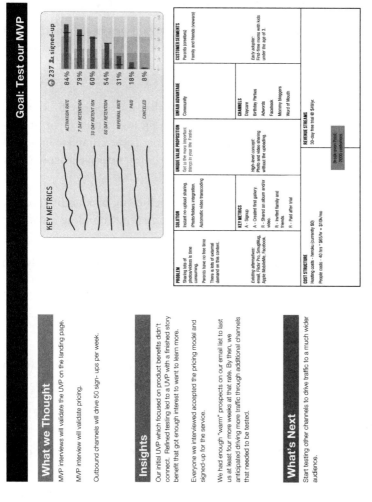

Figure 5-3. *Lessons learned*

It starts by identifying the key goal or metric at the top.

On the left, it summarizes your learning from a particular period, broken into sections describing what you expected to happen (your hypotheses), what actually happened (your insights), and what you are going to do next (future experiments).

This "learning" is kept in check on the right using a tactical view into your customer lifecycle (which we'll cover in depth later) and a strategic view into your business model assumptions.

Communicating progress in this way lets you stay grounded in learning while constantly iterating toward a plan that works.

Applying the Iteration Meta-Pattern to Risks

Risks are tackled through experiments. The terrain before product/market fit is riddled with qualitative learning; though you may be able to mitigate some risks, you can never completely eliminate them through a single experiment.

There are two common fallouts of this. One is that startups get discouraged from their initial lukewarm or negative learning and either pivot prematurely or abandon further experiments. The other is the complete opposite. Here, startups get overly optimistic from their initial positive learning only to get potentially stuck later.

The first significant milestone of a startup is achieving product/market fit, which isn't just about building the *"right" product* but building *a scalable business model* that works.

You can't afford to blindly follow a process (even this one) or aimlessly run experiments just for the sake of learning. Instead, you need to start with the end in mind and carefully align your experiments into "staged iterations" so that your learning is additive.

Maximize learning (about what's riskiest) per unit time.

The starting point is a completed Lean Canvas that lays out a plan that you believe *should work*. You then methodically run staged experiments that visit every box on the canvas.

Your business model is not a dartboard.

Earlier, I outlined the top three starting risks on the Lean Canvas as Problem, Channels, and Revenue streams.

While the top three starting risks serve as a quick diagnostic for prioritizing your canvases, here is how you systematically tackle them in stages (see Figure 5-4):

Stage 1: Understand the problem

> Conduct formal customer interviews or use other customer observational techniques to understand whether you have a problem worth solving. Who has the problem, what is the top problem, and how is it solved today?

Stage 2: Define the solution

Armed with knowledge from Stage 1, take a stab at defining the solution, build a demo that helps the customer visualize the solution, and then test it with customers. Will the solution work? Who is the early adopter? Does the pricing model work?

Stage 3: Validate qualitatively

Build your MVP and then soft-launch it to your early adopters. Do they realize the unique value proposition (UVP)? How will you find enough early adopters to support learning? Are you getting paid?

Stage 4: Verify quantitatively

Launch your refined product to a larger audience. Have you built something people want? How will you reach customers at scale? Do you have a viable business?

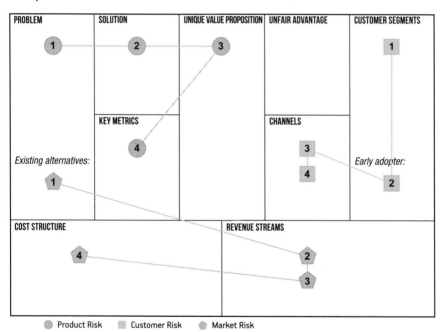

Figure 5-4. *Systematically eliminate risk*

Here is how you view them based on risks:

Product risk: Getting the product right

1. First make sure you have a problem worth solving.

2. Then define the smallest possible solution (MVP).

3. Build and validate your MVP at small scale (demonstrate UVP).

4. Then verify it at large scale.

Customer risk: Building a path to customers

1. First identify who has the pain.

2. Then narrow this down to early adopters who really want your product now.

3. It's OK to start with outbound channels.

4. But gradually build/develop scalable inbound channels—the earlier the better.

Market risk: Building a viable business

1. Identify competition through existing alternatives and pick a price for your solution.

2. Test pricing first by measuring what customers say (verbal commitments).

3. Then test pricing by what customers do.

4. Optimize your cost structure to make the business model work.

What About Unfair Advantage?

The only box not tackled is the Unfair Advantage box. This is because your true unfair advantage can only be tested in the face of competition. Until you demonstrate product/market fit, you most likely won't attract much (if any) competition.

So until then, embrace obscurity—it's a gift.

PART 4

SYSTEMATICALLY TEST YOUR PLAN

CHAPTER 6

Get Ready to Interview Customers

The fastest way to learn is to talk to customers. Not releasing code, or collecting analytics, but talking to people. We'll be using customer interviews as a learning tool[1] throughout the rest of book. This chapter lays some groundwork for conducting good interviews.

No Surveys or Focus Groups, Please

When asked to do the smallest thing to learn from customers, many founders' first instinct is to conduct a bunch of surveys or focus groups. While running surveys and focus groups may seem more efficient than interviewing customers, starting there is usually a bad idea.

Here's why:

Surveys assume you know the right questions to ask.

It is hard, if not impossible, to script a survey that hits all the right questions to ask, because you don't yet know what those questions are. During a customer interview, you can ask for clarification and explore areas outside your initial understanding.

Customer interviews are about exploring what you don't know you don't know.

---

1 In *The Four Steps to the Epiphany*, Steve Blank points out the importance of in-depth customer interviews, which he terms "Customer Discovery."

Worse, surveys assume you know the right answers, too.

In a survey, not only do you have to ask the right questions, but you also have to provide the customer with the right choice of answers. When taking a survey, how many times has your best answer been "Other"?

The best initial learning comes from "open-ended" questions.

You can't see the customer during a survey.

Body language cues are as much an indicator of Problem/Solution Fit as the answers themselves.

Focus groups are just plain wrong.

The problem with focus groups is that they quickly devolve to "group think," which is wrong for most products.

Are Surveys Good for Anything?

While surveys are bad at supporting initial learning, they can be quite effective at verifying what you learn from customer interviews.

I discussed the principle of two-phase validations earlier—*first qualitative, then quantitative.* The customer interview is a form of qualitative validation that is quite effective in uncovering strong signals for or against hypotheses using a "reasonably" small sample size.

Once you have preliminary validation on your hypotheses, you can then use what you have learned to craft a survey and verify your findings quantitatively. The goal is no longer learning, but demonstrating scalability (or statistical significance) of the results.

But Talking to People Is Hard

The customer development battle cry, *"Get out of the building,"* codified by Steve Blank, is simultaneously one of the most basic and difficult practices to implement.

People assume talking to customers came easy for me, which is simply not true. (They also assume I live in Silicon Valley, which is also not true.)

Like most other technical founders, I too was a closeted geek. I used tools like email, discussion forums, and product blogs for years to avoid having to talk directly to customers. When I did talk to customers, the conversations either didn't feel productive or sent me off on wild goose chases.

I knew listening to customers was important, but I didn't know how.

I went from dreading direct customer interaction to wiring my mobile phone to a toll-free number. The pivotal turning point for me occurred when I realized: *"Life is too short to keep building something nobody (or not enough people) want."*

This coincided with my early exposure to customer development and Lean Startups that jump-started my own rigorous testing and application of these principles.

While customer development makes a compelling, albeit rational, argument for talking to customers, getting our bodies to listen to our heads is nonetheless challenging at first.

"Go talk to a customer" is about as useful as "Build something people want." The big question is: *What do you say to them?*

Here are some tactics for overcoming your initial mental blocks:

Build a frame around learning, not pitching.

> In a pitch, since you're doing most of the talking, it's very easy for customers to pretend to go along with what you're saying, or to outright lie to you.

> The problem with starting with a pitch is that it is predicated on having knowledge about the "right" product for the customer (Problem/Solution Fit).

> *Before you can pitch the "right" solution, you have to understand the "right" customer problem.*

> In a learning frame, the roles are reversed: you set the context, but then you let the customer do most of the talking. You don't have to know all the answers, and every customer interaction (interview, tech support, feature request, etc.) turns into an opportunity for learning. Plus, people are generally willing to help if you set the right expectation of seeking their advice over trying to pitch to them.

Don't ask customers what they want. Measure what they do.

> It's fairly common to find customers lying in interviews—sometimes out of politeness and sometimes because they really don't know or don't care enough.[2] Your job shouldn't be to call out their lies, but rather to find ways to validate what they say with what they do, preferably during the interview.

---

2 This is also called observer bias (or the Heisenberg and Hawthorne bias), where the mere act of observing customers makes them change their behavior.

For example, if a customer declares a problem as a must-have, probe deeper. Ask him how he solves the problem today. If he is doing nothing and still getting by, the problem may not be as acute. If, however, he is using a homegrown or competitor's solution and he is not happy, that may be a problem worth solving.

Another tactic is to use strong calls to action. If a customer says he would pay for your product, instead of getting just a verbal commitment, ask for an advance payment or partial payment and provide him with a money-back guarantee.

We'll cover several other tactics later in the book.

Stick to a script.

While exploration is a critical aspect of talking to customers, you need to bind the conversation around specific learning goals. Otherwise, you can easily blow off a lot of time and end up with an overwhelming amount of unactionable information.

Unlike a pitch, it doesn't help to tweak your story after every interview. You need consistency and repeatability to instill some method to the process. Scripts help you do that.

I'll share actual scripts I use for each type of interview in the next chapter.

Cast a wider net initially.

Even though your first objective will be to home in on the defining attributes of early adopters, not all of your prospects will (or should) be early adopters. It's better to start with a broader sweep of initial prospects at this stage (to avoid running into a local-maxima problem), and refine from there. You will have ample opportunity to narrow down your filter in the next round of interviews.

> *Recruit loosely and grade on a curve.*
> —*Steve Krug,* Rocket Surgery Made Easy *(New Riders Press)*

Prefer face-to-face interviews.

Earlier, I stressed the importance of being able to see your interviewees. In addition to picking up on body language cues, I find that meeting someone in person instills a sense of closeness that you can't re-create virtually. This is critical in customer relationship building.

Start with people you know.

Finding people to interview can be challenging at first. Start with people you know who fit your target customer profile. Then use them to get two or three degrees out to find other people to interview. Not only does this help you practice and get comfortable with your script, but it's an effective way to get warm introductions to other prospects.

Take someone along with you.

It always helps to have one other person in the room during the interview to make sure nothing slips through the cracks. But more important, it helps to keep the learning objective.[3]

I conducted my first problem interview for CloudFire with my wife. I also asked her to tag along with me during subsequent interviews, which not only helped me connect better with other moms but also served as a constant reality check along the way.

Pick a neutral location.

I prefer to conduct the first interview in a coffee shop to create a more casual atmosphere. Doing it at a prospect's office makes it more "business-like" and makes it feel more like a sales pitch—which it shouldn't be. That being said, I'll agree to meet the prospect wherever she chooses.

Ask for sufficient time.

My interviews typically run between 20 and 30 minutes, without feeling rushed. Make sure you set the right time expectations up front and are respectful of the interviewees' time.

Don't pay prospects or provide other incentives.

Unlike usability testing, where it is acceptable to provide incentives for participation, your goal here is to find customers who will pay you, not the other way around.

Avoid recording the interviewees.

I tried recording interviewees early on (with their permission), but found that it made some people self-aware during the interview— another example of observer bias. That, coupled with the fact that I never really went back to listen to an interview, made it a nonstarter for me. Your mileage may vary.

Document results immediately after the interview.

I recommend spending five minutes immediately following an interview to document the results while your thoughts are fresh. Debrief with others later.

---

3 Entrepreneurs are typically optimistic by nature and easily susceptible to the expectancy bias—seeing what they want to see.

Prepare yourself to interview 30 to 60 people.

As a rule of thumb, prepare to interview 30 to 60 people over a four- to six-week period, which means talking to two or three customers a day, with some time built in for iteration.

The actual numbers could vary based on the strength of the signal you receive, your specific path to customers, and your business model. You know when you are done: when you stop learning anything new from the interviews. In other words, when you can accurately predict what the customer is going to say just by asking a few qualifying questions, you are done.

Consider outsourcing interview scheduling.

The biggest source of waste during this period is waiting—waiting for people to get back to you, coordinating around their schedules, juggling time zones, and so on. If you do a little up-front work, you might be able to successfully delegate this task to someone else (like a virtual assistant).

Here's how I have made this work:

- I script all my email requests for interviews.

- I clear my afternoons so that it's easy to schedule interviews.

- I'm copied in all the emails so that I can intervene when needed.

Finding Prospects

Whenever possible, you want to prioritize finding prospects through a channel you will actually use to acquire future customers. Unless you already have a path to customers, this may not be possible at this stage.

Here is a list of other techniques you can use to find and recruit interviewees:

Start with your first-degree contacts.

The first place to start is with your immediate contacts that meet your target customer demographic. Some are wary that feedback received from close contacts may be biased. My view is that *talking to anyone is better than talking to no one.*

Ask for introductions.

The next step is to ask your first-degree contacts for introductions to people who meet your customer demographic. It's a good idea to include a message template that your contacts can simply cut and paste and forward to save them time. Here's an example:

Hey [friend],

Hope all is well... I have a quick favor to ask.

I've got a product idea that I'm trying to validate with wedding photographers. My goal is to chat with local photographers to better understand their world and evaluate whether it's worthwhile pursuing this product.

I'd really appreciate it if you could **send this message** along to people you know who fit this target.

(Feel free to change it a bit if you like.)

Hello,

We are an Austin-based software company currently working on a new service to **simplify how photographers showcase and sell their images online**. Specifically, we are building better and faster tools for online proofing, archiving, and selling.

I would love to get **30 minutes of your time** to help us understand your current workflow. **I'm not selling anything**, just looking for advice.

Thanks,

Ash

Play the local card.

People are generally willing to meet if they can identify with you. The email in the preceding list item emphasizes "Austin" in the body and was quite effective in setting up meetings with local photographers.

Create an email list from the teaser page.

If the Web is a viable channel for your product, setting up a teaser page early is a great way to find people to interview. See the Appendix for detailed steps on crafting a teaser page.

While you may not know whether people here meet your target customer demographic, they do represent people who were motivated enough to act on your unique value proposition (UVP). Reach out to them and ask if they'd be willing to spend 20 to 30 minutes with you on a call.

Give something back.

Turn the interview into a "real interview" and offer a write-up, blog post, or video in exchange.

Use techniques such as cold calling, emailing, and LinkedIn.

The secret to getting a prospect (cold or warm) to agree to an interview is to *"nail their problem."* You may not be able to do that out of the gate, which is why I typically rely on the other techniques in this list to run a few interviews first.

Preemptive Strikes and Other Objections (or Why I Don't Need to Interview Customers)

Let me address some common objections to the idea of interviewing customers:

"Customers don't know what they want."

It is not your job to ask your customers for a list of features. Rather, it's to understand their problems and solve them with a compelling solution.

"Talking to 20 people isn't statistically significant."

A startup is about bringing something bold and new into the world. Your biggest challenge at first will be to get anyone to pay attention.

When 10 out of 10 people say they don't want your product, that's pretty significant.

—Eric Ries

Once you can get 10 people to repeatedly say yes, you're in a much better position.

"I only rely on quantitative metrics."

Another commonly used tactic is to sit back and rely solely on quantitative metrics. The first problem with this approach is that initially you probably won't have or be able to buy enough traffic. But more important, metrics can only tell you what actions your visitors are taking (or not); they can't tell you why this is happening. Did they abandon your website because of bad copy, graphics, pricing, or something else? You could endlessly try various combinations, or you could just ask the customers.

"I am my own customer, so I don't need to talk to anyone else."

The 37signals folks advocate building products for yourself (scratching your own itch) as the best way to build a successful product. While I agree that is an advantage since you start with a problem you've experienced firsthand, it's not an excuse for not talking to customers. For starters, can you really be that objective about the problem and pricing?

While you might share the same problems with your potential customers, the fact that you are also an entrepreneur automatically *disqualifies you as a customer.* Even if you think you are building products for other entrepreneurs who share the same worldview as you, *you have to test that.*

Scratching your own itch is a great way to get started, but you still need to validate that you have a problem worth solving by talking to other people.

"My friends think it's a great idea."

I advocate talking to anyone at first, but the point isn't to get objective learning. Your family and friends may paint a rosier picture (or not) depending on their perceptions of entrepreneurship as a profession. Instead, use your friends to practice your script, and find more people to interview that are a few degrees out.

"Why spend weeks talking to customers when I can build something over a weekend?"

"Release early, release often" was a mantra that software developers jumped on several years ago as a means to facilitate faster feedback, but spending any time building even this "small" release can be time wasted.

First, these "small" releases are almost never "small" enough. But more important, you don't need to finish building a solution in order to test it. Yes, you will need to help customers visualize your solution, but you don't need code or the actual product for that—proxies like mock-ups, physical prototypes, sketches, videos, and landing pages can fit the bill quite well. You have to challenge yourself to come up with the smallest possible solution in order to speed up learning.

"I don't need to test the problem, because it's obvious."

Problems may be obvious for a number of sometimes legitimate reasons:

- You have extensive prior domain knowledge.

- You are solving generally acknowledged problems, such as improving sales or conversion rates on a landing page.

- You are solving well-known but difficult problems, such as finding the cure for cancer or fighting poverty.

In these cases, the bigger risks may not have to do with testing the problem, but rather understanding the problem—that is, which customers are most affected (early adopters), how they solve these problems today (existing alternatives), and what you would offer that is different (UVP).

Even in these cases, I still recommend running a few Problem interviews to validate your understanding of the problem and then moving on to the Solution interviews.

"I can't test the problem, because it isn't obvious."

You might be building a product that you think isn't designed to solve a problem—for example, a video game, a short film, or a fiction novel. I argue that even in these cases there are underlying problems, albeit more desire- than pain-driven.

As in the previous case, I agree that these don't need to be explicitly tested. Instead first spend time understanding your audience (early adopter) and then look for smaller, faster ways to test your solution—for example, build a teaser trailer for your video game, short film, or book.

"People will steal my idea."

The initial interviews (and teaser pages) should be entirely problem-focused, where you are seeking to understand problems from customers who already know they have them. So there's nothing to steal here.

It's not until the Solution interviews that you start revealing your solution. By then you should have qualified those early adopters who most likely would rather pay for your solution than build one themselves.

That being said, it's equally important to remember that your sustainable advantage will come from your ability to outlearn your current (and future) competition.

"People won't buy vaporware."

When you are able to nail the customer's problem and help him visualize a viable solution, he will buy from you, provided that you remove other objections—for example, by providing a trial period, making it easy to cancel, and so on.

Selling a product is fundamentally about risk mitigation.

With my latest product, USERcycle, I used only customer interviews, HTML, and Illustrator mock-ups to understand the problem, define the solution, and sign up 100 paying customers before I started building the MVP. We'll cover how to do this in Chapter 8.

CHAPTER 7

The Problem Interview

Understand your customer's worldview before formulating a solution.

What You Need to Learn

The Problem interview is all about validating your hypotheses around the "problem-customer segment" pair. In the Problem interview, you are specifically looking to tackle the following risks:

Product risk: What are you solving? (Problem)

> How do customers rank the top three problems?

Market risk: Who is the competition? (Existing Alternatives)

> How do customers solve these problems today?

Customer risk: Who has the pain? (Customer Segments)

> Is this a viable customer segment?

Testing the Problem

Your first objective is measuring how customers react to your top problems. Some ways of doing this are measuring customer reaction to a problem-centric teaser landing page,[1] blog post, or a Google/Facebook ad.

---

1   See the Appendix for how to create a teaser landing page.

While these tactics can be helpful in quickly gauging problem resonance with customers, you still need to engage customers more actively to truly understand the problems they face—specifically if/how they solve them today. This might be done using informal observation techniques like those employed in the "Design Thinking" and "User Centric Design" methodologies, and/or using structured customer interviewing techniques.

When faced with a new product idea, I typically prefer starting with some or all of the informal testing/observation techniques above to quickly gauge customer reaction, and then follow up with a more structured Problem Interview script, which we'll cover next.

For additional resources on these customer observation and interviewing techniques, I recommend checking out:

- *The Four Steps to Epiphany* by Steve Blank (*http://www.cafepress.com/kandsranch*)

- *Rapid Contextual Design* by Karen Holtzblatt, Jessamyn Wendell, and Shelley Wood (Morgan Kaufmann)

- *Human-Centered Design Toolkit* by IDEO (*ideo.com*)

CASE STUDY

Understand Problems Through Observation

After publishing the first edition of *Running Lean*, I set aside 2 hours a week for readers to set up a free 30-minute chat with me where they could ask me any question about their startup. The point of these calls wasn't to pitch them a solution or even get feedback about the book (which often surprised the callers), but simply to understand how other entrepreneurs approached their products and what problems they faced. These calls were instrumental in helping me identify recurring problem themes that led to more blog posts, more workshops, this book, and two products: Lean Canvas and USERcycle.

Formulate Falsifiable Hypotheses

To make the interview results actionable, you need to take an additional step to convert the hypotheses from your canvas into falsifiable hypotheses.

This process is best illustrated with an example.

CloudFire

Figure 7-1 shows my canvas from earlier, with the sections being tested highlighted.

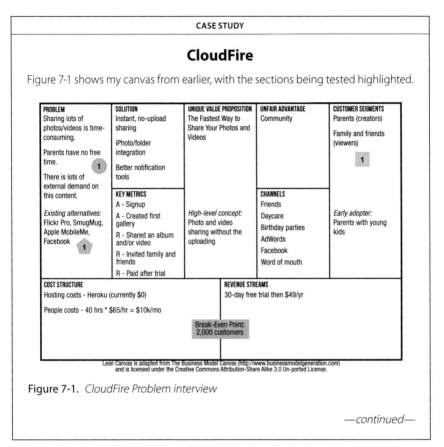

Figure 7-1. *CloudFire Problem interview*

—continued—

For each of these areas, I applied the falsifiable hypothesis formula to create the basis of my experiments (see Figure 7-2).

Falsifiable Hypothesis = [Specific Repeatable Action] will [Expected Measurable Action]

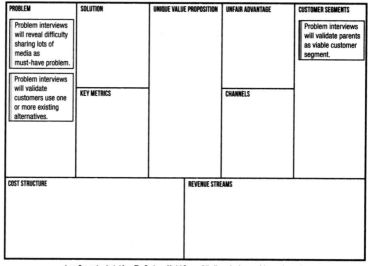

Lean Canvas is adapted from The Business Model Canvas (http://www.businessmodelgeneration.com) and is licensed under the Creative Commons Attribution-Share Alike 3.0 Un-ported License.

Figure 7-2. *CloudFire Problem interview experiments*

—— NOTE ——————————————————————

When you engage customers, it's fairly common to learn a lot more than you set out to test. We'll capture this additional knowledge more loosely (as insights) and reflect them onto our canvas at the end of the iteration.

Conduct Problem Interviews

Next, we'll walk through a Problem interview script that follows the structure shown in Figure 7-3.

PROBLEM INTERVIEW SCRIPT DECONSTRUCTED

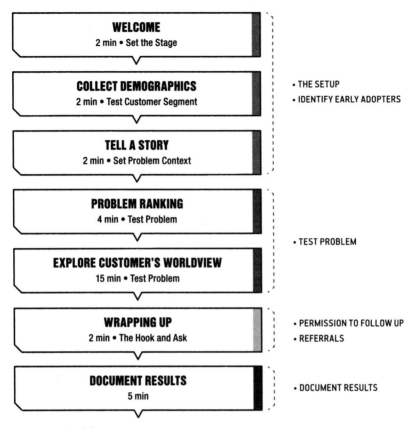

Figure 7-3. *Problem interview script*

Welcome (Set the Stage)

(2 minutes)

Briefly set the stage for how the interview works:

> Thank you very much for taking the time to speak with us today.

> We are currently working on a photo and video sharing service designed for parents. I got the idea for the service after recently becoming a parent and watching my wife get frustrated with existing solutions.

> But before getting too far ahead of ourselves, we wanted to make sure other parents share these problems and see whether this was a product worth building.

The interview will work like this. I'll start by describing the main problems we are tackling, and then I'll ask if any of those resonate with you.

I'd like to stress that we don't have a finished product yet, and our objective is to learn from you, not to sell or pitch anything to you.

Does that sound good?

Collect Demographics (Test Customer Segment)

(2 minutes)

Ask some introductory questions to collect basic demographics that you believe will drive how you segment and qualify your early adopters:

Before we go on to the problems, I'd like to learn a little about you:

- How many kids do you have?
- How old are they?
- Do you share photos online?
- Do you share videos online?
- How often?
- With whom?

Tell a Story (Set Problem Context)

(2 minutes)

Illustrate the top problems with a story:

Great, thanks. So, let me tell you about the problems we are tackling.

Once we had kids, we found ourselves taking a lot more photos than before, and especially more videos. We also started getting regular requests (as in, weekly) for updates from grandparents and other family members. But we found it difficult to share all this content on a regular basis because the process was too time-consuming and sometimes painful.

We had to organize the files, resize them, and babysit the upload process. Video was even more painful because we often had to convert the video first (transcode it) into a web-friendly format.

Like most other parents, we are sleep-deprived and don't have as much free time as before. Having kids has given us a whole new appreciation for free time and we'd much rather spend our time doing other things.

Does any of this resonate with you?

Problem Ranking (Test Problem)

(4 minutes)

State the top one to three problems and ask your prospects to rank them:

Specifically:

1. Do you find yourself taking more photos/videos than before?
2. Do you find the photo/video sharing process painful?
3. Are you like most parents in that you don't have a lot of free time?

Do you have any other photo- and video-sharing pet peeves I didn't talk about?

> ——— **NOTE** ———————————————————————
> So that you don't bias the ranking, frequently reorder the Problem list.

Explore Customer's Worldview (Test Problem)

(15 minutes)

This is the heart of the interview. The best script here is "no script."

Go through each problem in turn. Ask the interviewees how they address the problem today. Then sit back and listen.

Let them go into as much detail as they wish. Ask follow-up questions, but don't lead them or try to convince them of the merits of a problem (or solution).

In addition to their raw responses, judge their body language and tone to get a sense of how they'd rate the problem: "must-have," "nice to have," or "don't need."

If they offer up new problems along the way, explore them the same way:

1. So, how do you share photos and videos today?
2. Could you walk us through your workflow?
3. What products do you currently use and how did you first hear about them?

Ask any follow-up questions to understand their current workflow.

This section is invaluable both for understanding the problems and for confirming the prospects' earlier problem ranking. Sometimes people unknowingly lie to you during the problem rankings, either because they are being polite or they simply don't know. Check for that here. If they claim a problem is a "must-have," but they aren't actively doing anything to solve it, there's a disconnect.

Wrapping Up (the Hook and Ask)

(2 minutes)

We are done with all of the hypothesis-related questions, but you still have one more thing to do and two more questions to ask.

Even though you aren't ready to talk about your solution in detail, you need to provide a hook to maintain interest. The high-concept pitch is perfect for this. It not only helps explain your solution at a high level, but also leaves a memorable sound bite that helps the interviewees spread your message.

Then you need to ask for permission to follow up. Your goal is to establish a continuous feedback loop with prospects. And finally, you need to ask the interviewees for referrals to other potential prospects:

> As I mentioned at the start, this isn't a finished product, but we are building a product that will simplify how parents share their photos and videos online. The best way to describe the concept might be "SmugMug without any uploading" (replace "SmugMug" with the name of the interviewee's existing service).

> Based on what we talked about today, would you be willing to see the product when we have something ready?

> Also, we are looking to interview other people like yourself. Could you introduce us to other parents with young kids?

Document Results

(5 minutes)

Take the five minutes immediately following an interview to document your results while they're still fresh in your mind.

It helps to create a template like the one that follows so that you can quickly jot down the responses to the hypotheses you set out to test.

I recommended earlier that you run the interview with one other person whenever possible to keep the results objective. Each of you should independently fill out the form first. Then have a debriefing session later where you compare notes and make a final entry into whatever system you use to record your interview results.

PROBLEM INTERVIEW

Date: _____

Contact Information

Name: _____

Email: _____

Demographics

Number of kids: _____   Ages: _____

Shares photos online: _____   Shares videos online: _____

How often? _____   With whom? _____

Problem 1: Sharing lots of photos and videos is time-consuming.

   Priority ranking: _____   Pain level: _____

How problem is addressed today? _____

_____

Problem 2: There is a lot of external demand for this content.

   Priority ranking: _____   Pain level: _____

How problem is addressed today? _____

_____

Problem 3: I don't have enough free time for photo/video sharing.

   Priority ranking: _____   Pain level: _____

How problem is addressed today? _____

_____

Notes: _____

Referrals: _____

Do You Understand the Problem?

In this section, I'll discuss how to make sense of your interview results, refine the interview script, and determine when you are done.

Review your results weekly.

If you are scheduling interviews at a good pace, you should be talking to 10 to 15 people a week. Don't change the script during the week. Rather, debrief at the end of each week to review that week's batch of interviews, summarize your learning, and make any adjustments to your script.

The kinds of adjustments you make will vary based on the type of hypotheses you are testing and the strength of the signal you are getting from interviewees. The goal is to adjust the script and customer demographic along the way so that you can incrementally get stronger and more consistent positive signals with each subsequent batch.

Start to home in on early adopters.

Look for identifying demographics among the responses that were most favorable (i.e., strong problem resonance). Similarly, drop segments that were least favorable.

Refine the problems.

If you get a strong "don't need" signal across the board, drop that problem from the script. Similarly, if you discover a new "must-have" problem, add it to the script. Your eventual goal is to distill your product down to one "must-have" problem—one Unique Value Proposition (UVP).

Really understand their existing alternatives.

Understanding your early adopters' existing alternatives is key to formulating the right product. Early adopters will use their existing alternatives as anchors against which they will judge your solution, pricing, and positioning. So, for instance, if their existing alternatives are all free, your product has to promise and deliver enough value to overcome the fact that the alternatives are free.

Pay attention to words customers use.

The best way to uncover the "key" words to use in your UVP is to listen closely to how customers describe their workflow.

Identify the potential paths to reaching early adopters.

Once you start getting a sense of who the early adopters are, start identifying the path to reach more people like them. We'll start testing these channels in Chapter 8.

What Are the Problem Interview Exit Criteria?

You are done when you have interviewed at least 10 people and you:

- Can identify the demographics of an early adopter
- Have a must-have problem
- Can describe how customers solve this problem today

CASE STUDY

CloudFire: Problem Interview Learning

After running 15 problem interviews with parents, we felt we had a good understanding of the problem.

Here's what we learned.

Product risk: What are you solving? (Problem)

Hypothesis

Problem interviews will reveal that difficulty in sharing lots of media is a must-have problem.

Insights

More than 80% of the interviewees expressed frustration with their current solution. We thought most of the frustration was going to be around the uploading process, but we learned that while uploading lots of photos was painful, people had implemented certain measures, such as selecting a few photos at a time to share. Asked whether they would share more if the process were simpler, most people said yes (a new hypothesis that would need to be tested).

A bigger pain seemed to exist around video sharing. A lot of parents weren't sharing videos today but wanted to. The biggest obstacle was that they did not know how to get started. Many had tried but gave up after they failed to get their videos transcoded (converted) correctly for web viewing.

—continued—

In addition to these insights, simply listening to parents describe their existing work-flow uncovered a whole host of other problems, captured in the workflow diagram shown in Figure 7-4.

Pain points in parents photo/video sharing workflow

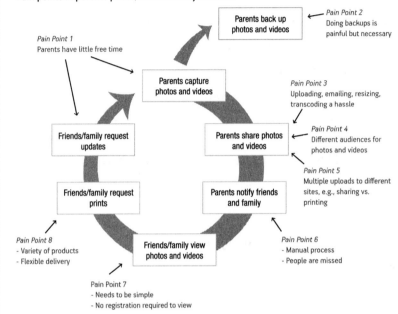

Figure 7-4. *CloudFire pain points*

One that repeatedly stood out was the fear of losing all their photos and videos (currently only on their desktops) due to a lack of backups. We started testing this in subsequent Problem interviews and it resonated strongly with the other parents, too.

Market risk: Who is the competition? (Existing Alternatives)

Hypothesis

Problem interviews will validate our belief that customers use one or more of the existing alternatives (SmugMug, Flickr, MobileMe, Facebook, etc.).

Insights

Going into these interviews, we expected most parents to be using either Smug-Mug or Flickr, but we were surprised to learn that 60% of them used only email for photo sharing (see Figure 7-5).

—continued—

What We Thought

What We Learned

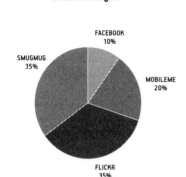
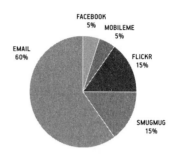

Figure 7-5. *Existing Alternatives learning*

When asked why this was so, they cited ease of use—interestingly, not for themselves, but for their viewers, typically grandparents. Despite the attachment size limits on email, everyone knew how to use email already.

Your customers' customers are your customers.

Customer risk: Who has the pain? (Customer Segment)

Hypothesis

Problem interviews will validate our belief in parents as a viable customer segment.

Insights

Eighty percent of parents expressed some form of frustration with their existing solutions, but 60% of them were currently getting by with a "free alternative": email. This posed a challenge, as we would need to justify the value of CloudFire against something that was free, and we uncovered several additional hypotheses that would need to be tested:

- A simpler sharing workflow would make parents share more content (including video).
- An automatic backup process would solve a big pain point for parents.
- Parents would pay $49 a year for this solution.

Updated Lean Canvas

Based on these insights, we updated our canvas with the changes shown in Figure 7-6.

—continued—

PROBLEM	SOLUTION	UNIQUE VALUE PROPOSITION	UNFAIR ADVANTAGE	CUSTOMER SEGMENTS
Sharing lots of photos/videos is time-consuming.	Instant no-upload sharing	The Fastest Way to Share Your Photos and Videos	Community	Parents (creators)
Don't know how to share (convert) videos.	Automatic video transcoding			Family and friends (viewers)
Afraid they will lose their media because it isn't backed up.	Cloud backups of originals			

	KEY METRICS		CHANNELS	
Existing alternatives: Email, Flickr Pro, SmugMug, Apple MobileMe, Facebook	A - Signup	*High-level concept:* Photo and video sharing without the uploading	Friends	*Early adopter:* Parents with young kids
	A - Created first gallery		Daycare	
	R - Shared an album and/or video		Birthday parties	
	R - Invited family and friends		AdWords	
	R - Paid after trial		Facebook	
			Word of mouth	

COST STRUCTURE	REVENUE STREAMS
Hosting costs - Heroku (currently $0)	30-day free trial then $49/yr
People costs - 40 hrs * $65/hr = $10k/mo	

Break-Even Point:
2,000 customers

Lean Canvas is adapted from The Business Model Canvas (http://www.businessmodelgeneration.com)
and is licensed under the Creative Commons Attribution-Share Alike 3.0 Un-ported License.

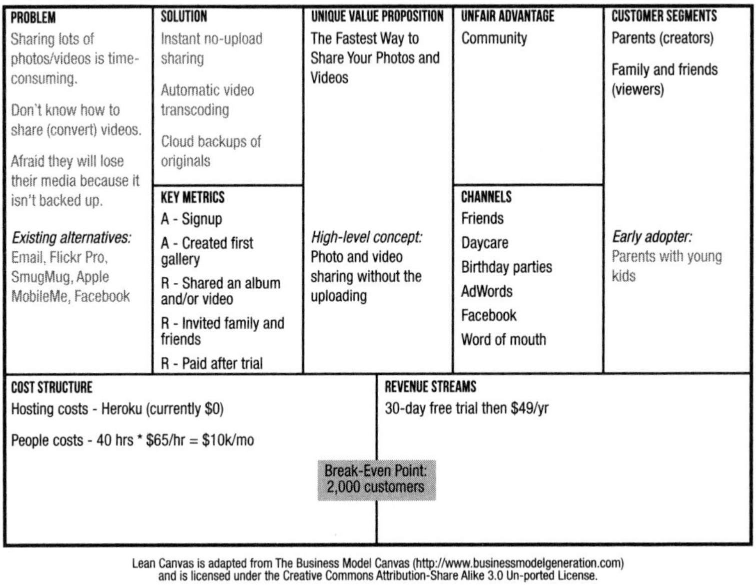

Figure 7-6. Updated Parents Lean Canvas

What's next?

Turning these insights into a demo and conducting Solution interviews.

CHAPTER 8

The Solution Interview

Test the solution with a "demo" before building the actual product.

What You Need to Learn

Armed with a prioritized problem list and an understanding of existing alternatives, you are now ready to formulate and test a solution.

You will start by double-checking your learning from the Problem interview, then look to test the following additional risks:

Customer risk: Who has the pain? (Early Adopters)

How do you identify early adopters?

Product risk: How will you solve these problems? (Solution)

What is the minimum feature set needed to launch?

Market risk: What is the pricing model? (Revenue Streams)

Will customers pay for a solution?

What price will they bear?

Testing Your Solution

The main objective here is to use a "demo" to help customers visualize your solution and validate that it will solve their problem.

Most customers are great at articulating problems but not at visualizing solutions.

I use the term *demo* loosely to mean anything that can reasonably stand in for the actual solution. The assumption here is that building the "full solution" is time-consuming and could lead to waste if you build the wrong solution or add unneeded features. You want to build just enough of the solution (or a proxy, like screenshots, a prototype, etc.) that you can put in front of customers for the purpose of measuring their reaction and further defining the requirements for your minimum viable product (MVP).

For software products, mock-ups and videos are a great way to "demo" your intended solution. Physical products could rely on sketches, computer-aided design (CAD) models, or even rapid prototypes built with clay or 3D printing.

Whatever medium you pick for your demo, keep these guidelines in mind:

The demo needs to be realizable.

>I have friends at design studios that have special teams in place just to build early user demos. These demos are very much a part of the sales process and a lot of emphasis is placed on them, but they often rely on technologies (like Flash) that aren't what the final product is built in. While they are quite effective at making the sale, they make the implementation team's job quite difficult—with many of the more "flashy" elements sometimes being impossible to re-create. This leads to a disconnect in what is promised (and sold) to the client and what is eventually delivered.

The demo needs to look real.

>I also don't like going to the other extreme of relying on barebones wireframes or sketches. While they are faster to put together, they require the customer to take a leap of faith on the finished product, which I try to avoid.

>*The more real your demo looks, the more accurately you'll be able to test your solution.*

The demo needs to be quick to iterate.

>You will probably get valuable usability feedback during the interviews that you'll need to quickly incorporate and test in subsequent interviews. This is where outsourcing your demo to an external team could actually hurt you if your ability to iterate is driven by their schedule.

The demo needs to minimize waste.

>Creating a mock-up in anything other than the final technology in which the product will be delivered creates some waste. For my mockups, although I start rapid prototyping using paper sketches, Photoshop, and Illustrator, at some point I convert them into HTML/ CSS, which results in less waste in the long run.

The demo needs to use real-looking data.

Instead of using "dummy data" (e.g., *lorem ipsum* text), come up with "real-looking" data that not only will help you lay out your screen but will also support your solution narrative.

Content precedes design. Design in the absence of content is not design, it's decoration.
       —*Jeffrey Zeldman,* A List Apart *(Happy Cog Studios)*

CASE STUDY

CloudFire

In the case of CloudFire, I strung together a few screens and built a video that demonstrated how a user could share 500 photos from existing photo albums in iPhoto and 10 movies from a desktop folder in less than two minutes.

As before, there are techniques for quickly gauging initial reaction to a potential solution—for example, by posting a demo video to your landing page or blog and measuring engagement with it (like Dropbox did). Here too, I prefer starting with these techniques as a quick litmus test, but rely on more structured customer interviews for validation.

CASE STUDY

Testing a Solution Using a Blog Post

In August 2009, I published a blog post titled "How I Document My Business Model Hypotheses." I had been following Steve Blank's approach for capturing business model hypotheses using worksheets as described in his book, but I was struggling with keeping them updated. From conversations with other Customer Development practitioners, I knew others had the same problem.

I had come across Alex Osterwalder's work on the Business Model Canvas prior to that but had originally dismissed the canvas approach as too simple. Seeing another entrepreneur, Rob Fitzpatrick, create a variation that combined Steve Blank's worksheets with Alex Osterwalder's canvas inspired me to do some tinkering of my own. The result was Lean Canvas, which I described in this post.

The post quickly rose to become one of my most popular posts of all time. I interpreted this as a strong signal favoring this approach and used this momentum to line up several formal customer interviews that further validated the merits of this solution. That eventually led to recruiting a team[1] (also through my blog) to build the online version of Lean Canvas.

---

1   Lukas Fittl, Ross Hale, Andrew Elliott

Testing Your Pricing

I find that people often misunderstand the "learning versus pitching" metaphor for customer interviews. Yes, your objective in customer interviews is to learn, not to sell, but you can't learn effectively when you're too vague or open-ended.

You have to go into interviews with clear falsifiable hypotheses that may very well be shattered. That's OK.

What you intend to charge for your product is one such hypothesis, but how you test it is a little different. Unlike a "must-have" problem hypothesis where you attempt to uncover an inherent "truth about customer behavior" through probing, pricing is a lot more "gray" and needs to be tackled more directly.

Don't Ask Customers What They'll Pay, Tell Them

Can you imagine Steve Jobs asking you what you would have been willing to pay for an iPad before it launched? Sounds ludicrous, right? Yet, you've probably asked a customer for a "ballpark price" at some point.

Well, that's just backward. Think about it. There is no reasonable economic justification for a customer to offer anything but a low-ball figure. Customers might honestly not know how much they'd pay, and this question only makes them uncomfortable.

You can't (and shouldn't) convince a customer that she has a must-have problem, but you often can (and should) convince a customer to pay a "fair" price for your product that is usually higher than what both you and the customer think it is.

The mindset most of us have during Solution interviews is one of *"lowering signup friction."* We want to make it as easy as possible for customers to say yes and agree to take a chance on our product, hoping the value we deliver over time will earn us the privilege of their business.

Not only does this approach delay validation because it's too easy to say yes, but a lack of strong customer "commitment" can also be detrimental to optimal learning.

Your job is to find early adopters who are at least as passionate about the problems you're addressing as you are, and if you're charging, who are willing to pay your fair price. As we covered earlier, your pricing not only is part of your product, but it also defines the customer segment you attract.

Don't Lower Signup Friction, Raise It

I know this may run counter to your intuition. It did with mine. Here's a social experiment I ran during one of my customer interviews (and have repeated several times since then) that changed my perspective.

I had just finished demonstrating the solution and verified that we had a real "must-have" problem and solution on our hands.

> *Me: So, let's talk about pricing...*
>
> *Customer: Do we need to negotiate pricing right away?*
>
> *Me: This is not really a negotiation. While we have been using this product internally ourselves, we need to justify whether it's worth productizing externally.*
>
> *Customer: Oh, OK.*
>
> *Me: So, what would you pay for this product?*
>
> *Customer: I don't know—probably something in the range of $15 to $20 a month.*
>
> *Me: Well, that's not the pricing we had in mind. We want to start with a $100/month plan. I can understand why you don't want to pay a lot (because you are pre-revenue), and it's possible that we'll offer a freemium or starter plan in the future.*
>
> *Right now, we are specifically looking for 10 [define early adopters] who clearly have a need for [state top problem]. We will work closely with these 10 companies to validate [state unique value proposition (UVP)] within 30 to 60 days or give them their money back.*
>
> *You mentioned that you've spent several developer hours a month building a homegrown system and still haven't been happy with the results. This product is our third attempt; $100/month is less than two developer hours a month.*
>
> *Customer: Yes, that makes a lot of sense. We want to be on the shortlist. I can justify paying $1,200/year. It's just a fraction of what we pay our developers. How do we get on the list?*
>
> *Me: We're still finalizing some product details and I'll get back to you once we're ready.*
>
> *Customer: We seriously want to be part of the initial customer list. I'll run upstairs and get my checkbook if you want me to...*

So, what happened there? Why did the customer agree to pay five times the original amount?

There were a number of principles in play, summarized as follows:

Prizing

> Oren Klaff discusses this framing technique in his book, *Pitch Anything* (McGraw-Hill). He describes how, in most pitches, the presenter plays the role of a jester entertaining in a royal courtyard (of customers). Rather than trying to impress, position yourself to be the prize.

Scarcity

> The "10 customer" statement was not a fake ploy. The first objective with your MVP is to learn. I'd much rather have 10 "all-in" early adopters I can give my full attention to than 100 "on-the-fence" users any day.[1]

Anchoring

> As we covered earlier, price is relative. However, while pricing against "existing alternatives" might seem logical to you, customers might not automatically make the reference themselves. Even Steve Jobs used this principle when he introduced pricing for the iPad in a brand-new category. He skillfully anchored iPads against pundit predictions (who used netbooks for price anchors) and made the iPad look like a steal.

Confidence

> Most people are reluctant to charge for their MVP because they feel it's too "minimal," and they might even be embarrassed by it. I don't subscribe to this way of thinking. The reason for painstakingly testing problems and reducing scope is to build the "simplest" product that *solves a real customer problem.*

The Solution Interview as AIDA

AIDA is a marketing acronym for Attention, Interest, Desire, and Action, and a useful framework for structuring Solution interviews. Here's how:

Attention

> Get the customer's attention with your UVP—derived from the number-one problem you uncovered during earlier Problem interviews.
>
> *The most effective way to get noticed is to nail a customer problem.*

---

1 The 10X Product Launch: *http://www.ashmaurya.com/2011/10/the-10x-product-launch/*

Interest

Use the demo to show how you will deliver your UVP and generate interest.

Desire

Then take it up a notch. When you lower signup friction, you make it too easy for the customer to say yes, but you are not necessarily setting yourself up to learn effectively. You need to instead secure strong customer commitments by triggering on desire. The earlier pricing conversation generated desire through scarcity and prizing.

Action

Get a verbal, written, or prepayment commitment that is appropriate for your product.

How Is This Different from a Pitch?

While this might look a lot like a pitch, the framing is still around learning.

A pitch tends to be an all-or-nothing proposition. Here, you lead with a clear hypothesis at each stage and measure the customer's reaction. If you fail to elicit the expected behavior at each stage, it's your cue to stop and probe deeper for reasons. For instance, you might have your positioning wrong or be talking to the wrong customer segment.

The AIDA framework used here is also applicable when designing your future landing page or other sales collateral. Over time, you tend to rely on other elements like social proof, brand, and so on to generate desire, but never underestimate the power of incorporating strong emotional triggers.

Formulate Testable Hypotheses

Once again, you need to document the testable hypotheses you intend to test during the interview.

CloudFire

Figure 8-1 shows our canvas from earlier with the sections being tested highlighted. Figure 8-2 shows the basis of my experiments.

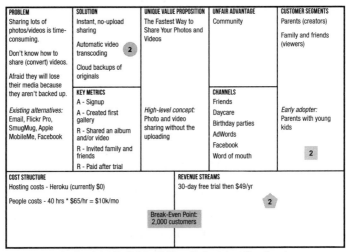

PROBLEM	SOLUTION	UNIQUE VALUE PROPOSITION	UNFAIR ADVANTAGE	CUSTOMER SEGMENTS
Sharing lots of photos/videos is time-consuming. Don't know how to share (convert) videos. Afraid they will lose their media because they aren't backed up.	Instant, no-upload sharing Automatic video transcoding **2** Cloud backups of originals	The Fastest Way to Share Your Photos and Videos	Community	Parents (creators) Family and friends (viewers)
Existing alternatives: Email, Flickr Pro, SmugMug, Apple MobileMe, Facebook	**KEY METRICS** A - Signup A - Created first gallery R - Shared an album and/or video R - Invited family and friends R - Paid after trial	*High-level concept:* Photo and video sharing without the uploading	**CHANNELS** Friends Daycare Birthday parties AdWords Facebook Word of mouth **2**	*Early adopter:* Parents with young kids **2**
COST STRUCTURE Hosting costs - Heroku (currently $0) People costs - 40 hrs * $65/hr = $10k/mo		**REVENUE STREAMS** 30-day free trial then $49/yr **2** Break-Even Point: 2,000 customers		

Lean Canvas is adapted from The Business Model Canvas (http://www.businessmodelgeneration.com) and is licensed under the Creative Commons Attribution-Share Alike 3.0 Un-ported License.

Figure 8-1. *CloudFire Solution interview*

PROBLEM	SOLUTION	UNIQUE VALUE PROPOSITION	UNFAIR ADVANTAGE	CUSTOMER SEGMENTS
	Solution interviews will validate minimum feature set.			Solution interviews will validate first-time moms with kids under the age of 3 as early adopters.
	KEY METRICS		**CHANNELS**	
COST STRUCTURE		**REVENUE STREAMS** Solution interviews will drive verbal commitments to pay $49/yr for service.		

Lean Canvas is adapted from The Business Model Canvas (http://www.businessmodelgeneration.com) and is licensed under the Creative Commons Attribution-Share Alike 3.0 Un-ported License.

Figure 8-2. *CloudFire Solution interview experiments*

Conduct Solution Interviews

You're now ready to conduct the Solution interview:

Use old prospects.

You should have received permission to follow up from your earlier Problem interviews. If the prospects match your early-adopter demographic, arrange a follow-up Solution interview with them.

Mix in some new prospects.

It's a good idea to mix in new prospects with every batch of interviews so that you test all the hypotheses with a "beginner's mind." Your earlier interviews should have yielded some referrals that you can use. This is also the time to start testing any other channels you identified in your last iteration.

Next, we'll walk through a Solution interview script using the structure shown in Figure 8-3.

SOLUTION INTERVIEW SCRIPT DECONSTRUCTED

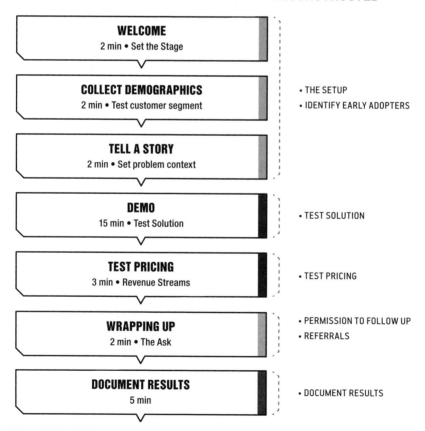

Figure 8-3. *Solution interview script*

Welcome (Set the Stage)

(2 minutes)

As before, you need to briefly set the stage for how the interview works:

> Thank you very much for taking the time to speak with us today.

> We are currently working on a photo and video sharing service designed for parents. I got the idea after becoming a parent and experiencing some frustrations firsthand with existing solutions.

> The interview will work like this. I'll start by describing the main problems we are tackling and then I'll ask whether any of those resonate with you. I also would like to show you an early demo of the application.

> I'd like to stress that we don't have a finished product yet, and our objective is to learn from you, not to sell or pitch anything to you.

> Does that sound good?

Collect Demographics (Test Customer Segment)

(2 minutes)

Ask some introductory questions to collect basic demographics that you believe will drive how you segment and qualify your early adopters. If you've already interviewed this prospect, you can skip this section unless there are additional questions you've uncovered since you last interviewed him.

> Before we go on to the problems, I'd like to learn a little about you:

> - How many kids do you have?

> - How old are they?

> - Do you share photos online?

> - Do you share videos online?

> - How often?

> - With whom?

Tell a Story (Set Problem Context)

(2 minutes)

As before, illustrate the top three problems with a story:

Great, thanks. So, let me tell you about the problems we are tackling.

Once we had kids, we found ourselves taking a lot more photos than before, and especially more videos. We also started getting regular requests (as in, weekly) for updates from grandparents and other family members. But we found it difficult to share all this content on a regular basis because the process was too time-consuming and sometimes painful.

We had to organize the files, resize them, and babysit the upload process. Video was even more painful because we often had to convert the video first (transcode) into a web-friendly format.

Like most other parents, we are sleep-deprived and don't have as much free time as before. Having kids has given us a whole new appreciation for free time, and we'd much rather spend our time doing other things.

Does any of this resonate with you?

If you don't sense a strong problem resonance, don't continue with the Solution interview, but rather use the Problem interview script to learn more about how the prospects solve these problems today.

Demo (Test Solution)

(15 minutes)

This is the heart of the interview.

Go through each problem in turn and illustrate how you solve it using the supporting demo.

<For each problem>

Illustrate how you solve the problem using the supporting demo.

Pause after each one and ask if they have any questions.

<Repeat for other problems>

So, that's what the application looks like right now. We are trying to prioritize what to finish and release first and would like to ask you a few more questions:

- What part of the demo resonated with you the most?

- Which could you live without?

- Are there any additional features you think are missing?

Test Pricing (Revenue Streams)

(3 minutes)

Finding the right price is more art than science.

Usually the right price is one the customer accepts, but with a little resistance.

Test pricing using the "starting price" you determined earlier for this customer segment.

Don't ask the customer for ballpark pricing. Instead, tell him your pricing model (with or without anchoring) and gauge his response immediately afterward. If he accepts the pricing, make a note of whether he hesitated or readily accepted.

So, let's talk about pricing next.

We will launch the service using a subscription model.

Would you pay $49 a year for unlimited photo and video sharing?

Wrapping Up (the Ask)

(2 minutes)

We are done with all the hypothesis questions, but you still have two more questions to ask.

The first is permission to follow up with them to test the service when it's ready. If possible, try to secure a more concrete commitment than just a verbal one.

The second is to ask for referrals to other people you could potentially interview.

Thanks a lot for your time today. You have been very helpful.

As I mentioned at the start, this isn't a finished product, but we are close to launching something soon. Would you be interested in trying out the product when we have something ready?

Also, we are looking to interview more people like yourself. Do you know any other parents of young kids who we could interview?

Document Results

(5 minutes)

Take the five minutes immediately following an interview to document your results while they're still fresh in your mind.

It helps to create a template like the one that follows so that you can quickly jot down the responses to the hypotheses you set out to test.

As before, have each interviewer independently fill out the form first. Then have a debriefing session later where you compare notes and make a final entry into whatever system you use to record your interview results.

SOLUTION INTERVIEW

Date: _____

Contact Information

Name: _____

Email: _____

Demographics

Number of kids: _____   Ages: _____

Shares photos online: _____   Shares videos online: _____

How often? _____   With whom? _____

Solution: Instant, no-upload sharing

    Priority ranking: _____   Pain level: _____

Additional comments: _____

Solution: iPhoto/folders integration

    Priority ranking: _____   Pain level: _____

Additional comments: _____

Solution: Automatic video transcoding

    Priority ranking: _____   Pain level: _____

Additional comments: _____

Pricing

Willing to pay ($X/month): _____

Notes: _____

Referrals: _____

Do You Have a Problem Worth Solving?

In this section, I'll discuss how to make sense of your interview results, refine the interview script, and determine when you are done.

Review your results weekly.

> As before, wait until you have a week's worth of interviews to change the script.

Add/kill features.

> If you received specific usability or feature enhancements, discuss whether there were compelling reasons to incorporate them. Remove unnecessary features.

Confirm your earlier hypotheses.

> If you ended your Problem interview iteration with strong positive signals, there should be no surprises here. Otherwise, revisit your older hypotheses and refine them until you get consistent results.

Refine pricing.

> If you got no resistance to your pricing, consider testing a higher price. Take the customers' alternative solutions into account. If their current solution is free, how can you provide more value to justify them paying for your solution?

> Again, look for patterns. Who are the prototypical early adopters and what price will they bear? Can you build a viable business at that price?

What Are the Solution Interview Exit Criteria?

You are done when you are confident that you:

- Can identify the demographics of an early adopter
- Have a must-have problem
- Can define the minimum features needed to solve this problem
- Have a price the customer is willing to pay
- Can build a business around it (using a back-of-the-envelope calculation)

CloudFire: Solution Interview Learning

After running another 20 Solution interviews, here's what we learned:

Customer risk: Who has the pain? (Early Adopters)

Hypothesis

Solution interviews will validate parents with young kids as early adopters.

Insights

Based on earlier responses, we observed that moms typically did most of the sharing and that the motivation to share was highest with the first child in the family, which also translated to family members. We also noticed that some sharing fatigue set in once the child was more than three years old.

In subsequent interviews, we were able to further narrow our early-adopter definition to *"first-time moms with kids under the age of three."* This was very useful, as it made the process of identifying and targeting our early adopters much simpler.

Product risk: How will you solve these problems? (Solution)

Hypothesis

Solution interviews will validate the minimum feature set.

Insights

The demo we showed was very well received and conveyed the speed and ease of sharing. The fact that originals got backed up as a side effect of sharing really hit home. While many parents requested specific third-party app integration (into iPhoto, Picasa, etc.), they were OK about starting with a folder-based sharing model. Our rationale for starting there was that it required less work (than building custom integrations into third-party apps) and it was universal (every desktop has a filesystem).

Market risk: What is the pricing model? (Revenue Streams)

Hypothesis

Solution interviews will drive verbal commitments to pay $49/year.

Insights

As expected, parents with "free alternatives" were a little resistant to pricing, but they did see value in backing up their files by way of sharing and agreed to a trial. Parents who were already paying for a service had no reservations about paying, provided that we made it simple to migrate their existing content to CloudFire.

—continued—

Updated Lean Canvas

Based on the refined early-adopter definition, we identified a few more potential channels, shown in Figure 8-4.

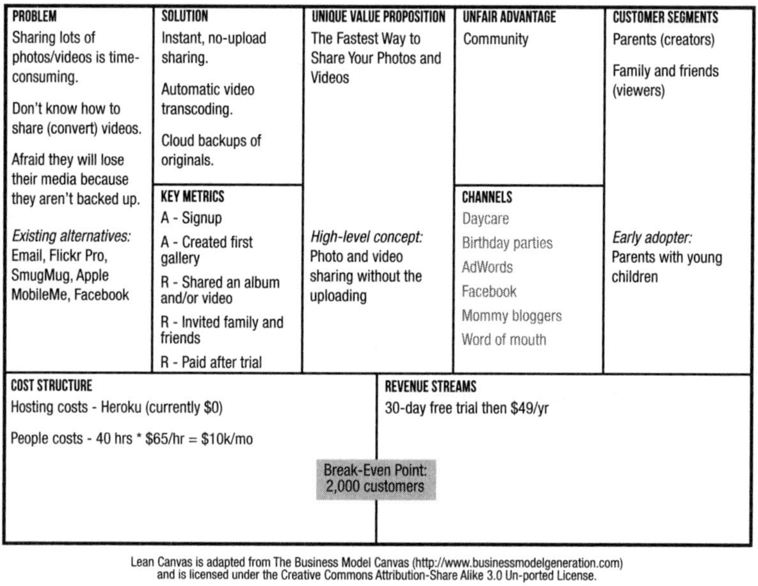

PROBLEM	SOLUTION	UNIQUE VALUE PROPOSITION	UNFAIR ADVANTAGE	CUSTOMER SEGMENTS
Sharing lots of photos/videos is time-consuming. Don't know how to share (convert) videos. Afraid they will lose their media because they aren't backed up.	Instant, no-upload sharing. Automatic video transcoding. Cloud backups of originals.	The Fastest Way to Share Your Photos and Videos	Community	Parents (creators) Family and friends (viewers)
Existing alternatives: Email, Flickr Pro, SmugMug, Apple MobileMe, Facebook	**KEY METRICS** A - Signup A - Created first gallery R - Shared an album and/or video R - Invited family and friends R - Paid after trial	*High-level concept:* Photo and video sharing without the uploading	**CHANNELS** Daycare Birthday parties AdWords Facebook Mommy bloggers Word of mouth	*Early adopter:* Parents with young children
COST STRUCTURE Hosting costs - Heroku (currently $0) People costs - 40 hrs * $65/hr = $10k/mo		**REVENUE STREAMS** 30-day free trial then $49/yr Break-Even Point: 2,000 customers		

Lean Canvas is adapted from The Business Model Canvas (http://www.businessmodelgeneration.com) and is licensed under the Creative Commons Attribution-Share Alike 3.0 Un-ported License.

Figure 8-4. *Updated Parents Lean Canvas*

What's next?

Use this learning to define and build the MVP.

CHAPTER 9

Get to Release 1.0

Reduce scope and shorten the cycle time between requirements and release so that you get to the learning parts faster.

Product Development Gets in the Way of Learning

Let's start by taking a closer look at where learning (about customers) happens during a typical product development cycle (see Figure 9-1).

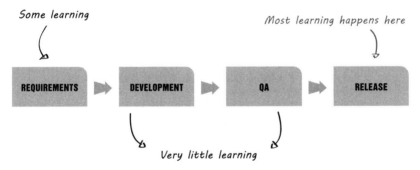

Figure 9-1. *Traditional product development cycle*

While some learning happens during the requirements-gathering stage, most learning happens after you release your product. Even though building a product is the purpose of a startup, very little learning happens during development and QA. Sure, you're learning about other things then, just not about customers.

We obviously can't eliminate development and QA, but we can shorten the cycle time from requirements to release so that you *get to the learning parts faster.*

The first step is to reduce the scope of your minimum viable product (MVP) to its essence so that you build the smallest thing possible.

Reduce Your MVP

A danger with iterating through mock-ups during the Solution interview is that it is quite easy to get carried away and end up with more than you need for your MVP. In order to reduce waste and speed up learning, you need to pare down your mock-ups so that all you have left is the essence of your product: your MVP.

Reducing the scope of your MVP not only shortens your development cycle, but also removes unnecessary distractions that dilute your product's messaging.

Your MVP should be like a great reduction sauce—concentrated, intense, and flavorful.

Here's how to do that:

1. Clear your slate.

   Don't automatically assume that any features have to be included in your MVP. Start with a clean slate and justify the addition of each one.

2. Start with your number-one problem.

   The job of your unique value proposition (UVP) is to make a compelling promise.

   The job of the MVP is to deliver on that promise.

   The essence of your MVP should be captured in the mock-up of your number-one problem. Start there.

3. Eliminate nice-to-haves and don't-needs.

   From your Solution interviews, you should be able to label every element on your mock-up as "must-have," "nice-to-have," or "don't need." Immediately eliminate the don't-needs, and add the nice-to-haves to your features backlog queue *unless* it is a prerequisite feature for a must-have feature.

4. Repeat Step 3 for your number-two and number-three problem mock-ups.

5. Consider other customer feature requests.

Your customers may have highlighted certain features that are needed to make your product complete or usable—for example, integration with Salesforce.com. Visit these next, and add/defer them based on the "must-have" level of need.

6. Charge from day one, but collect on day 30.

It is a given for products nowadays to have some sort of trial period. It is also generally a good practice to defer up-front collection of credit card information to reduce signup friction and avoid negative option billing.

Both of these work to your advantage to further reduce scope. You don't need to worry about merchant accounts, recurring subscription providers, or supporting multiple plans for launch. You'll have 30 days after launch to get these things working.

7. Focus on learning, not optimization.

All your energy needs to be channeled toward accelerating learning. Speed is key. Don't waste any effort trying to optimize your servers, code, database, and so on for the future. Chances are quite high that you *will not* have a scaling problem when you launch. In the rare event that you do (a great problem), most scaling problems can be initially patched with additional hardware that you can justify because you should be charging your customers—buying you time to address the problem more efficiently.

Get Started Deploying Continuously

Another technique for shortening the cycle time from requirements to release is implementing a Continuous Deployment process (see Figure 9-2).

Continuous Deployment is a practice of releasing software continuously throughout the day—in minutes versus days, weeks, or months.

Figure 9-2. *Continuous Deployment process*

Continuous Deployment is built on continuous flow techniques that were developed at Toyota. Continuous flow has been shown to boost productivity by rearranging manufacturing processes so that products are built end-to-end, one at a time, versus the more prevalent batch-and-queue approach.

The goal is to eliminate waste. The biggest waste in manufacturing is created from having to transport products from one place to another. The biggest waste in software is created from waiting for software as it moves from one state to another: waiting to code, waiting to test, waiting to deploy. Reducing or eliminating these wait times leads to faster iterations, which is the key to success.

Of all the Lean Startup techniques, Continuous Deployment is one of the most controversial. One of the immediate concerns that is usually raised concerns quality: comparing Continuous Deployment to "cowboy coding."

Implemented correctly, Continuous Deployment does *not* shortcut quality and actually demands much stricter testing and monitoring standards. Continuous Deployment is not just practiced by small startups; it is in use at larger companies like IMVU (one of the earliest pioneers), Flickr, and Digg. But among all the examples, Wealthfront is often used as the poster child for operating in a true mission-critical environment—deploying more than a dozen releases a day in a highly regulated SEC environment.

These companies collectively serve millions of users a day and have built fairly sophisticated Continuous Deployment systems to ensure high quality standards, which leads to the second concern.

The second concern usually raised is that building such a Continuous Deployment system is a massive and daunting undertaking. It is. But these systems were built incrementally over a span of years. As we'll see, the Continuous Deployment process is itself a feedback loop for continuous learning and improvement, which lends itself well to starting out small and is why I am covering it now.

Right now is the perfect time to lay the groundwork and practice with Continuous Deployment—while you don't have customers, lots of code, or servers to worry about. While Continuous Deployment won't help you launch your MVP faster, starting with a basic system won't slow you down and will help lay the foundation for speeding up future iterations after you launch.

It is also important to point out that while Continuous Deployment deploys code into production in small batches, this code does *not* have to be live for your users. There is a distinction between a "software release" and a "marketing release."

(See "How to Get Started with Continuous Deployment" in the Appendix.)

Define Your Activation Flow

Once you have distilled your features list, you are ready to start defining your activation flow.

Your activation flow describes the path customers take from signing up for your service to having a gratifying first experience.

The Anatomy of an Activation Flow

The activation flow is a subfunnel made up of the steps shown in Figure 9-3.

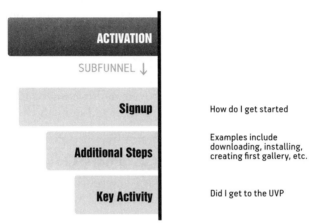

Figure 9-3. *Activation flow*

While the ultimate objective of your activation flow is to get your customers to experience your UVP as quickly as possible, most of what goes wrong right after you launch happens here.

For this reason, it is far more critical to architect your activation flow for learning over optimization.

Here are some ways to do that:

Reduce signup friction, but not at the expense of learning.

It is generally a good practice to keep your signup forms short and only collect what you absolutely need, but don't shy away from asking for critical contact information (like an email address) up front. (See the sidebar, "Have a Back Channel to Customers: CloudFire," for more on this.)

Forms are the least of our problems.
—*Joshua Porter, Bokardo* (Bokardo.com)

Reduce the number of steps, but not at the expense of learning.

The same principle of architecting for learning over optimization also applies to the number of steps in your activation flow. While it is important to reduce the number of steps, it is far more important to keep critical steps separate so that you can troubleshoot where people drop off when things go wrong. (See the sidebar, "Avoid Premature Optimization: Posterous [Blogging Platform]," for more on this.)

Deliver on your UVP.

A good activation flow needs to deliver on the promise established on your landing page. When you map out your activation flow, make sure it demonstrates your UVP—preferably in one sitting. You only get one chance to make a good first impression.

Be prepared for when things go wrong.

Offer inline troubleshooting and provide multiple ways customers can reach out for help: email, a 1-800 number, and so forth.

Have a Back Channel to Customers: CloudFire

CloudFire is a downloadable desktop application, and in the interest of simplifying the signup process, we put a simple Download button on the home page and deferred the account creation step to post-installation.

Our analytics showed a huge discrepancy between the number of downloads and the number of signups. We knew we were losing people during the installation step but didn't know why. At first, we tried implementing several hypotheses (best guesses), such as reducing the installer size, supporting an online installer, and so on, which took several weeks to implement but with no noticeable impact. Then we moved up the signup screen and started asking for an email address before the download step.

While this didn't fix the activation problem, it allowed us to identify the users that ran into these problems and reach out to them. Several of them responded, which helped us quickly uncover a few critical issues we hadn't caught before that were the key to solving our low activation rates.

Avoid Premature Optimization: Posterous (Blogging Platform)

In terms of keeping critical steps separate, an extreme example that comes to mind is the landing page on the Posterous website when it first launched. Rather than asking you to sign up for an account, they asked you to email them a message with the contents of your first post (see Figure 9-4). While this was a novel idea, they were essentially asking you to "abandon" their landing page to send an email, which treated an activated user the same way as an uninterested visitor. This flow, while highly optimized, offered little opportunity for learning when things went wrong.

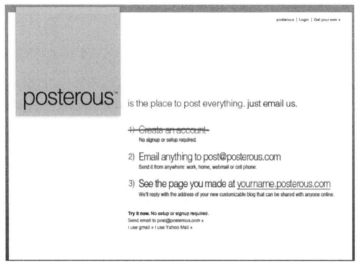

Figure 9-4. *Posterous screenshot*

Build a Marketing Website

The purpose of your marketing website is simple: *to sell your product.*

Your marketing website is critical in driving the acquisition trigger in your customer lifecycle.

Acquisition describes the path a customer takes from first landing on your website as an unaware visitor to becoming an interested prospect.

The Anatomy of a Marketing Website

Acquisition is itself a subfunnel (see Figure 9-5).

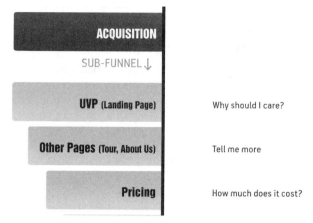

Figure 9-5. *Acquisition subfunnel*

Following the principle of architecting for learning over optimization, I recommend starting with explicit pages for each step. Each page should have a primary call to action and a secondary call to action. My primary call to action directs visitors to my pricing page (acquisition subgoal), while my secondary call to action offers a link to more information (e.g., product tour).

The landing page is by far the hardest of the three. Its job is to make a case for your product to an unaware visitor in fewer than eight seconds. We'll deconstruct the elements of a good landing page shortly, but first I'll list a few other pages you probably should also include:

About page

> While the job of your landing page is to provide a compelling reason to buy your product, the job of your About page is to provide a compelling reason to buy from your company. This is your opportunity to put a face on your product, to tell your story, and to connect with your customers.

Terms of Service and Privacy Policy pages

> Both of these pages are basic requirements for offering a service on the Web. They are also fairly standard, with lots of good examples online to model after. That said, the Terms Of Service and Privacy Policy can create legal headaches if they are not adequate. Put in at least enough time researching this part of your site to satisfy yourself that you are relying on decent models. If you have doubts, you should get some competent professional advice.

Tour page (video/screenshots)

I usually defer this page to later and start with just the landing page. But if your customers are more analytical or research-oriented, you might need to provide a separate page with more details, technical specifications, and so forth.

It comes down to fundamentally understanding your customers and their motivations.

The Landing Page Deconstructed

While the landing page has the daunting task of very quickly connecting with your visitors, there are several basic elements that make up a successful landing page, listed here and shown in Figure 9-6:

Unique value proposition

Put the latest refinement of your UVP here. This is the most important element of the page.

Supporting visual

Support your UVP with a visual aid that resonates strongly with your target audience. The actual medium may be an image, a screenshot, or a video depending on your specific audience.

A clear call to action

Every page needs to have a single, clear call to action. It should stand out and set a clear expectation as to what happens next.

Invitation to learn more

Some visitors may need more information before they're convinced. Provide additional links to your tour page (if you have one), or your 1-800 number.

Figure 9-6. Landing page elements

The landing page shown in Figure 9-6 is missing one critical element:

Social proof

Social proof elements help to raise your credibility and trust. They are typically provided through customer testimonials and "As Seen On" logos. The reason they are absent from the landing page in Figure 9-6 is that you don't have these yet and will get them later from your early adopters.

CHAPTER 10

Get Ready to Measure

You need not only the ability to visualize your customer lifecycle, but also the ability to measure it.

The Need for Actionable Metrics

Even though the terrain before product/market fit is riddled with qualitative learning, you still need actionable metrics to be able to visualize and measure your customer lifecycle.

The objective before product/market fit is *not* as much about optimizing for conversion and *all* about quickly identifying and troubleshooting hot spots in your customer lifecycle.

Up until now, you have made a number of product decisions based on what customers have told you. It's time to start measuring what they do.

What Is an Actionable Metric?

An actionable metric is one that ties specific and repeatable actions to observed results.

The opposite of actionable metrics are vanity metrics (like web hits or the number of downloads), which only serve to document the current state of the product but offer no insight (by themselves) into how you got there or what to do next.

A warning flag that indicates you might have a vanity metric on your hands is when the numbers don't go anywhere but up and to the right every month.

Put another way, things like web hits or downloads are elements of sub-funnels that make up the larger macro metric that matters, such as acquisition and activation.

It's not what you measure, but how.

Understanding the difference between a vanity metric and a macro metric is the first step. In order to make your metrics actionable, you have to additionally make them accessible (through simple reports) and auditable (by being able to go behind the numbers).

> *The three A's of metrics are: Actionable, Accessible, and Auditable.*
> —*Eric Ries*

I'll go into some detail regarding how you do that in the next few sections, and then I'll outline the steps for building a conversion dashboard.

Metrics Are People First

Eric Ries popularized the meme of "metrics are people too" for the purpose of making your metrics auditable, but I don't believe it goes far enough.

While I am a big proponent of building a metrics-driven culture, there is a lot more to building a great product than numbers. For starters, *you have to be able to go to the people behind the numbers.*

The ideal conversion dashboard is part analytics and part customer relationship management.

Here's why:

Metrics can't explain themselves.

> When you first launch a product or new feature, lots of things can and do go wrong. Metrics can help you identify where things are going wrong, but they can't tell you why. You need to talk to people for that.

Don't expect your users to come to you.

> When users first use your product, they aren't yet invested in your solution. They usually start out interested, but they are skeptical and their motivation decays quickly when things go wrong. In other words, you can't expect users to promptly send in a bug report or pick up the phone and call you when they need help. They might do this, but it's more likely that they'll simply abandon your product and leave. The burden of quickly identifying problems and reaching out to your users is yours.

Not all metrics are equal.

You've been very selective about who you've interviewed up until now. Once you launch, you won't be able to control who uses your product. In addition to your target early adopters, you might be visited by bots, curious onlookers, and maybe even other undiscovered target customers. When you just look at numbers, you get an averaging effect that can be greatly skewed if you don't yet have a lot of traffic (or the right traffic). You need a way to segment your metrics into different buckets.

Simple Funnel Reports Aren't Enough

The funnel report is a powerful analysis tool. It's simple to understand and lends itself well to visually depicting a conversion dashboard. But most third-party implementations of funnel reports are better suited at tracking micro-level funnels, like landing page conversions, than macro-level funnels, like your customer lifecycle.

Micro-level funnels are characterized by short lifecycle events typically measured in minutes, while macro-level funnels are characterized by long lifecycle events typically measured in days or months.

Simple funnel reports work by letting you specify a reporting period over which the number of key event occurrences are counted and visualized. This approach doesn't work when the intervals between events fall outside the reporting period.

To illustrate these problems, let's consider an example for a downloadable product that uses a 14-day trial.

Figure 10-1 shows an example of what a typical funnel report might look like.

Conversion Funnel for June

Figure 10-1. *Typical funnel report*

In Figure 10-1, the "acquisition" and "activation" events are short lifecycle events, while the "revenue" event is a long lifecycle event.

This poses the following issues:

Inaccurate conversion rates

> The numbers reported for the revenue event most likely include purchases made in May and exclude purchases made in July, which skews the overall conversion rates.

Dealing with traffic fluctuations

> This skewing of numbers is further exacerbated by any fluctuations in traffic. If signups go down in July, your conversion rates will appear to be better when they may not be.

Measuring progress (or not)

> Another problem with this sort of reporting is that your product is also constantly changing. It is hard, if not outright impossible, to tie back observed results (good or bad) to actions you took in the past, such as launching a new feature.

Segmenting funnels

> Over time, you will probably run a split test or need to segment your funnel to isolate one group of customers from another. You can't do this with a simple funnel report.

Say Hello to the Cohort

So, while funnels are a great visualization tool, funnels alone are not enough. The answer is to couple funnels with cohorts.

Cohort analysis is very popular in medicine, where it is used to study the long-term effects of drugs and vaccines:

> *A cohort is a group of people who share a common characteristic or experience within a defined period (e.g., are born, are exposed to a drug or a vaccine). Thus a group of people who were born on a day or in a particular period, say 1948, form a birth cohort. The comparison group may be the general population from which the cohort is drawn, or it may be another cohort of persons thought to have had little or no exposure to the substance under investigation, but otherwise similar. Alternatively, subgroups within the cohort may be compared with each other.*[1]

---

1 *http://en.wikipedia.org/wiki/Cohort_study*

We can apply the same concept of the cohort or group to users and track their lifecycle over time. For our purposes, a cohort is any property that can be attributed to a user. The most common cohort used is "join date," but as we'll see, this could just as easily be the user's "plan type," "operating system," "gender," or something else.

Let's see how cohort reports overcome the shortcomings with simple funnel reports.

The weekly cohort report (by join date) shown in Figure 10-3 was generated using the same data used in the simple funnel report earlier (which I show again in Figure 10-2 for comparison).

Conversion Funnel for June

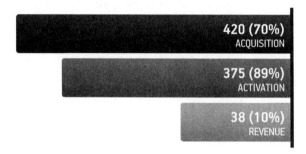

Figure 10-2. *Simple funnel report*

Conversion Funnel for June

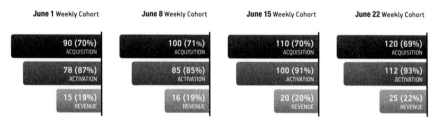

Figure 10-3. *Weekly cohort (by join date)*

You'll notice immediately that while the acquisition and activation conversion numbers are close enough, the revenue conversion rates are very different.

Dealing with traffic fluctuations

Since all the events are tied back to the users that generated them, cohort reports handle fluctuations in traffic correctly.

Measuring progress (or not)

More important, though, the weekly cohort report visibly highlights significant changes in the metrics, which can then be tied back to specific activities done in a particular week.

Segmenting funnels

Since cohort reports are inherently built around grouping users, they can be used to segment your funnels longitudinally around any property you track.

How to Build Your Conversion Dashboard

There are lots of third-party analytics products on the market. I have cut my teeth on Google Analytics, KISSmetrics, and Mixpanel. Each tool has its strengths and weaknesses, but unfortunately I haven't found a single analytics solution (yet) that addresses all the needs I outlined earlier.[2]

Rather than getting bogged down on the specifics of each tool, I cover how I built my conversion dashboard from a functional perspective in the Appendix.

---

2 USERcycle is my attempt at solving this problem.

CHAPTER 11

The MVP Interview

Before selling your minimum viable product (MVP) to strangers through your distribution channel (e.g., marketing website), sell it face to face to friendly early adopters. Learn from them. Then refine your design, positioning, and pricing for launch.

What You Need to Learn

With your MVP, marketing website, and conversion dashboard ready, you are all set to pay your prospects another visit. Your objective is to sign them up to use your service and, in the process, test out your messaging, pricing, and activation flow.

If you can't convert a warm prospect in a 20-minute face-to-face interview, it will be much harder to convert a visitor in less than eight seconds on your landing page.

During the MVP interview, you are specifically looking to answer the following questions:

Product risk: What is compelling about the product? (Unique Value Proposition or UVP)

Does your landing page get noticed?

Do customers make it all the way through your activation flow?

What are the usability hot spots?

Does your MVP demonstrate and deliver on your UVP?

Customer risk: Do you have enough customers? (Channels)

Can you bring on more customers using your existing channels?

Market risk: Is the price right? (Revenue Streams)

Do customers pay for your solution?

Formulate Testable Hypotheses

By now you should come to expect this step.

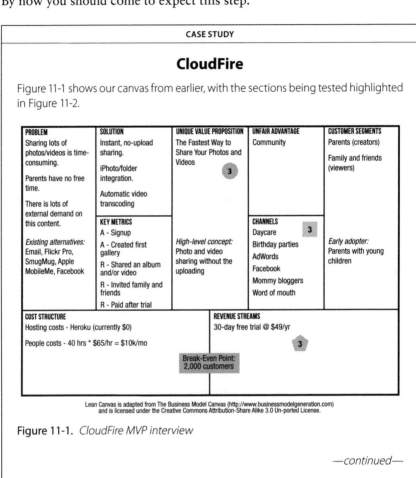

CASE STUDY

CloudFire

Figure 11-1 shows our canvas from earlier, with the sections being tested highlighted in Figure 11-2.

Figure 11-1. *CloudFire MVP interview*

—continued—

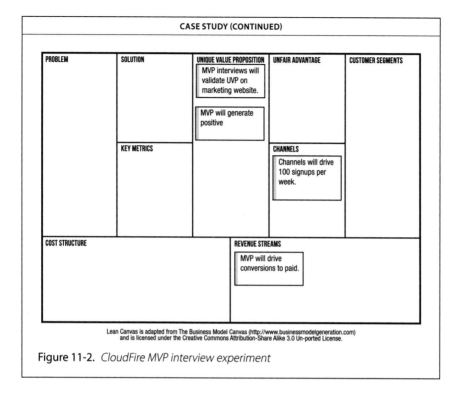

Figure 11-2. *CloudFire MVP interview experiment*

Conduct MVP Interviews

The MVP interview, like the Problem and Solution interviews, is less about pitching and more about learning. The structure of this interview largely follows a usability testing format described by Steve Krug in his book, *Rocket Surgery Made Easy* (New Riders Press). I highly recommend getting a copy of that book, as you'll be conducting a lot more usability tests in Part 4 of this book.

It is particularly important to conduct your initial MVP interviews in person. Over time, you might be able to do these with remote screen-sharing software.

If your entire team cannot be present during the interview, I recommend using screen-recording software (e.g., Camtasia, ScreenFlow) to record the testing session for others to watch later.

> *Watching usability tests is like travel: it's a broadening experience.*
> —Steve Krug, Rocket Surgery Made Easy *(New Riders Press)*

Next, we'll cover an MVP interview script using the structure shown in Figure 11-3.

MVP INTERVIEW SCRIPT DECONSTRUCTED

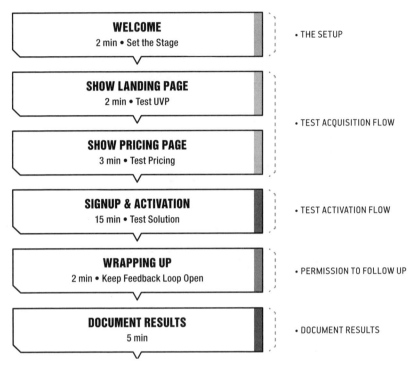

Figure 11-3. *MVP interview script*

Welcome (Set the Stage)

(2 minutes)

Briefly set the stage for how the interview works.

> Thank you very much for taking the time to meet with us again.

> We are almost ready to launch the photo- and video-sharing service we spoke about earlier. But before we launch, we wanted to show you the product, get your feedback, and, if you're still interested, give you early access to the tool.

> Does that sound good?

Great. We'd like to run the interview in a usability test format. So I'll start by showing you our website and asking you a few questions. It would be really helpful if you think out loud as we go along. That will help us identify any problems or issues we need to address.

Are you ready?

Show Landing Page (Test UVP)

(2 minutes)

Run a five-second test to test the site navigation/call to action.

OK, we'll start with the home page. Please take a look at the home page and tell us what you make of it. Feel free to look around, but don't click anything yet.

- Is it clear what the product is about?
- What would you do next?

Show Pricing Page (Test Pricing)

(3 minutes)

The interviewee should eventually end up on the pricing page, where you can then ask him about your pricing model.

Now, feel free to navigate anywhere on the site.

<When the interviewee navigates to the pricing page>

- This is the pricing model we decided to launch with.
- What do you think of it?

Signup and Activation (Test Solution)

(15 minutes)

This is the heart of the interview.

Ask the interviewee to sign up and watch how he navigates your activation flow.

- Are you still interested in trying out this service?
- You can do so by clicking the "Sign up" link.
- It would be immensely valuable to us if we could watch you go through the signup process. Would that be OK?

Wrapping Up (Keep Feedback Loop Open)

(2 minutes)

Hopefully, the interviewee made it all the way through and you have a list of usability issues to address.

Congratulations, you have your first user!

Make sure the user knows what to do next, and keep the conversation channel open with him.

> That's it. You're signed up and ready to go.
>
> What did you think of the process?
>
> Is there anything we could improve?
>
> Do you know what to do next?
>
> Thank you very much for your time today. If you have any questions or run into any issues, please call us or drop us a note.
>
> Would it be OK if I check in with you after you've had some time to use the tool some more—say, in a week?
>
> Great. Thanks again.

Document Results

(5 minutes)

As before, take the five minutes immediately following the interview to document your results while they're still fresh in your mind.

Use the following template to write down the top three problems you observed.

Have each person fill out this form independently and debrief later.

MVP INTERVIEW

Date: _____

Contact Information

Name: _____

Email: _____

Usability Problem 1

_____

_____

_____

Usability Problem 2

_____

_____

_____

Usability Problem 3

_____

_____

_____

Pricing

Willing to pay ($X/month): _____

Notes: _____

Referrals: _____

CHAPTER 12

Validate Customer Lifecycle

Now that you have some early customers signed up, work closely with them to ensure that they make it through your conversion funnel completely.

Make Feedback Easy

The fastest way to learn from customers is to talk to them.

Much like I favor interviewing customers over conducting surveys, I prefer getting feedback from customers in person or over the phone than through other means like email, forums, or discussion boards.

Here's why:

It shows you care.

A toll-free number sends a signal to your customers that you care and that you went the extra mile to make it easy for them to call you.

You don't have a scaling problem yet.

Contrary to popular belief, you won't be bombarded with phone calls. A lot of my calls are typically from prospects with questions about the service, not about support issues. It is fairly easy to set calling hours during the day and reroute the calls if and when you run into a scaling problem (which is a great problem to have).

Tech support is a continual learning feedback loop.

After each call, I review the reason for the call and see if I can change something on the site—messaging, help, tips, pricing clarifications, and so on—to continually improve the product.

Tech support is customer development.

Not only does talking to a customer help you better understand customer problems, but it provides you an opportunity to ask your customers a question or two.

Tech support is marketing.

The opportunity to learn from customers in this way is so great that I have my mobile phone tied to the 1-800 number of all my products.

Having the founder of the company answer the phone further shows your commitment to listening to customers, and I've found it empowers customers to open up even more.

It avoids voter-based feedback tools.

I'm not a fan of voter-based tools like GetSatisfaction and UserVoice because I don't believe all customers are equal. Listening to the most vocal or popular feedback does not guarantee you'll uncover the right learning to build a better product. More often than not, it can have the exact opposite effect.

Troubleshoot Customer Trials

I particularly like trials because they time-box the full customer lifecycle and force an outcome that leads to quick, actionable learning. Properly conducted trials are a goldmine of opportunity for learning, but they can just as easily be fumbled. The way to troubleshoot your trials is to follow the path a user takes through your customer lifecycle (see Figure 12-1).

Your first objective during trials is to reduce user abandonment on your acquisition and activation paths. Your next objective is to increase retention and engagement, get paid (if that applies), and collect favorable customer testimonials.

Your goal should be to get 80% of your early adopters through the complete cycle. Because you've manually qualified your early adopters until now, this number needs to be higher than what you might typically expect after you publicly launch your product.

GOALS

ACQUISITION	User is interested (views pricing page)
ACTIVATION	User signs-up and completes key activity
RETENTION	User comes back and uses the product
REVENUE	User converts to paying customer
REFERRAL	[Can be deferred for now]

Figure 12-1. *Customer trials*

Acquisition and Activation

Priority: Ensure that you are driving enough traffic to support learning.

Drill into your subfunnels.

Explore your acquisition and activation subfunnels to see where users are dropping off.

Start with the leakiest bucket first. Are you losing them on a particular page, such as the landing page or pricing page?

Look for patterns. Do certain types of users (e.g., Mac versus Windows users) experience higher failure rates than others?

Reach out to your users.

You should be able to extract the list of users that failed at a particular step in your funnel. If you know what went wrong, correct it, and ask those users to come back. If you don't know what went wrong, reach out with an offer for help (more like a call for help).

Catch and report unexpected errors.

When early users run into problems, they don't turn into testers. They leave. To be able to still learn from their experience, catch and report unexpected errors so that you can troubleshoot the problem without them.

Retention

Priority: Get users to come back and use your product during the trial.

Send gentle email reminders.

Email is a very effective (and often underutilized) medium for engaging your customers. Everyone has an email address. Email can be automated, tracked, and measured.

A common technique used by email marketers is *drip marketing,* where you schedule a set of predetermined messages to your users over time. Even interested users get busy and distracted, and gentle reminders can help bring them back to your product.

But even better than drip marketing is *lifecycle marketing.* Lifecycle marketing additionally considers the user's stage in the customer lifecycle. So, for instance, if a user gets stuck during activation, instead of educating him about your advanced features, you would know to send him timely and appropriate troubleshooting help.

Follow up with your interviewees.

During the MVP interview, you asked for permission to follow up with your early adopters. Follow through. Call them up or meet with them and get their feedback.

Revenue

Priority: Get paid.

Implement a payment system.

Now is the time to implement a payment system for customers to pay you.

Get paying customers to talk to you.

Get them on the phone, thank them for upgrading, and ask them:

- How they heard about you (if you don't know)

- Why they bought from you

- What could be improved

Get "lost sales" prospects to talk to you.

You stand to learn as much (if not more) from your lost sales as you do from your sales. While some people are happy to provide honest feedback if you make a sincere request at the end of the trial, others might need a small incentive. Offer a $25–$50 gift card or donation to charity in exchange for 15 minutes of their time.

Don't spend a lot of effort acquiring customers and then just let them walk away.

—Gary Vaynerchuck

Referral

Priority: Get testimonials.

Ask for customer testimonials.

Get happy customers to write a short paragraph on your product's value proposition.

Are You Ready to Launch?

In this section, I'll discuss how to determine when you are ready to open your product to the world.

1. Review your results frequently.

   Usability testing research shows that you can uncover 85% of your product's problems with as few as five testers.

2. Start with the most critical problems.

   Review everyone's top three problems and rank them by severity.

3. Do the smallest thing possible.

   Resist the temptation to completely redesign a new landing page or signup flow at this stage. Your objective is to first establish a baseline that works, and you can get there by making smaller tweaks. You'll have lots of opportunities to test alternate hypotheses in Part 4 of this book.

4. Make sure things improve.

   Validate that your fixes actually improve things in subsequent interviews. Repeat Steps 1–3.

5. Audit your conversion dashboard.

   This is the perfect opportunity to audit your conversion dashboard and make sure everything works as expected.

What Are the Launch Criteria?

You are ready when at least 80% of your early adopters consistently make it through your conversion funnel.

Specifically, they should:

- Be able to clearly articulate your unique value proposition (UVP)
- Be primed to sign up for your service
- Accept your pricing model
- Make it through your activation flow
- Provide positive testimonials

3, 2, 1 ... Launch!

Once you have a minimum viable product (MVP) that works, your final step is to revisit your acquisition channel(s) to ensure that you have a steady stream of prospects entering your funnel. However, be wary of spending a lot of effort prematurely optimizing your acquisition channels at this stage.

Strive to drive this traffic through the actual channels you've identified for your product (e.g., content marketing), but supplement with other means if needed (e.g., search engine marketing).

Your goal is to establish "just enough" traffic to support learning.

If you have a large list of "warm" prospects from your earlier efforts (teaser page, referrals from interviewees), consider exhausting that list first in the form of more "early access" signups before doing a public launch.

CASE STUDY

CloudFire: MVP Learning

We knew the photo- and video-sharing market was already crowded, which made it particularly important for us to validate our UVP. The first challenge to overcome with the UVP is "getting noticed." We used these interviews to test our UVP by showing people our landing page and measuring their reactions.

Product risk: Does the product deliver on value? (UVP)

Hypothesis

MVP interviews will validate the UVP on the landing page.

Insights

Iteration 1: Benefit hook

We started by showing moms the landing page depicted in Figure 12-2.

—continued—

Figure 12-2. *CloudFire landing page, iteration 1*

The feedback we received was that this didn't look "different enough" from existing services. Most moms felt their service was fast enough until we brought to their attention the fact that we used the word *instantly*, which meant we helped them share hundreds of photos/videos in "zero time." We learned that the word *instant*, like countless other marketing terms, carried no weight with prospects and was ignored. I even did a Google search afterward and found the following ad, which drove this point home:

Some Photo Printing Service

Get your photos printed while you wait.

Instantly in 30 minutes.

Even though we had a carefully orchestrated two-minute demo video link on the site, when a headline didn't connect with visitors, they didn't stick around to watch the video. We confirmed this with other usability tests we ran on UserTesting.com (which is an online usability testing service).

Iteration 2: Word hook

Next, we knew that words matter, so we made the targeted customer segment (Busy Parents) prominent in the headline and added a "No Uploading Required" splash burst to the screenshot in the hopes of attracting attention (see Figure 12-3).

Figure 12-3. *CloudFire landing page, iteration 2*

—continued—

The splash burst definitely caught viewers' attention and we got two types of reactions—both bad.

When a technical person encountered the "No Uploading Required" splash burst, he challenged that claim. We would then spend five minutes explaining how the product worked using a peer-to-web (p2web) model to achieve instant sharing without uploading.

When a nontechnical person encountered the "No Uploading Required" splash burst, he would get confused and ask how the product works. We'd have to spend five minutes again giving a less technical explanation.

The reason both reactions were bad is that you don't have five minutes on a landing page. When people don't trust you, they leave. So, even though we could have added a "how it works" page or graphic on the landing page, chances are people wouldn't stick around long enough to notice it.

Iteration 3: Emotional hook

Rather than trying to present a particular benefit or explain how the product works, we took a more aspirational tack; one that used an image to connect with the target customer and communicated a finished story benefit (see Figure 12-4).

Figure 12-4. *CloudFire landing page, iteration 3*

This version worked. The first reaction we got from moms was: "That's my life." That connection made them more open to reading the lefthand side of the page, which further connected with them by making the promise: "Get back to the more important things in your life. Faster." That piqued their interest enough to want to learn more, which is exactly what you want out of your UVP headline.

UVP: Why you are different and worth paying attention to.

—continued—

Qualitative versus quantitative learning

Interestingly, this experiment in landing pages also serves as a great example of showing how qualitative learning can trump quantitative learning in the early stages of a product. While we were interviewing moms, I also started an A/B split-test using Google Website Optimizer, driving traffic using Facebook ads, Google AdWords, and StumbleUpon.

CloudFire was the product I used to rigorously test Lean Startup techniques, and here I was pitting qualitative interviewing, which seemed like more effort, against quantitative metrics, which was much easier to conduct.

Through the interviews, we were able to conclusively declare iteration 3 as the winner within a week and after just 10 interviews. Not only did we know which version worked, but importantly, we knew why. All the insights mentioned earlier came directly from the parents we interviewed.

The quantitative A/B split-test, on the other hand, was still inconclusive after the third week. We eventually decided to cut the testing short because 100% of the moms we interviewed told us they had found their existing solution through a referral. They hadn't actively searched for a photo/video sharing solution, which made us further question the validity of testing these pages via ads. Who were these people clicking through the ads?

Market risk: Is the price right? (Revenue Streams)

Hypothesis

MVP interview will validate pricing.

Insights

Everyone we interviewed accepted the pricing model and signed up for the service.

Customer risk: Do you have enough customers? (Channels)

Hypothesis

Outbound channels will drive 50 signups per week.

Insights

We had enough "warm" prospects on our email list to last us at least four more weeks at that rate. By then, we anticipated driving more traffic through additional channels that needed to be tested.

Updated Lean Canvas

Figure 12-5 depicts the updated Lean Canvas.

—continued—

PROBLEM	SOLUTION	UNIQUE VALUE PROPOSITION	UNFAIR ADVANTAGE	CUSTOMER SEGMENTS
Sharing lots of photos/videos is time-consuming. Don't know how to share (convert) videos. Afraid they will lose their media because they aren't backed up. *Existing alternatives:* Email, Flickr Pro, SmugMug, Apple MobileMe, Facebook	Instant, no-upload sharing. Automatic video transcoding. Cloud backups of originals.	Get to the more important things in your life. Faster. *High-level concept:* Photo and video sharing without the uploading	Community	Parents (creators) Family and friends (viewers)
	KEY METRICS A - Signup A - Created first gallery R - Shared an album and/or video R - Invited family and friends R - Paid after trial		**CHANNELS** Daycare Birthday parties AdWords Facebook Mommy bloggers Word of mouth	*Early adopter:* Parents of young children

COST STRUCTURE	REVENUE STREAMS
Hosting costs - Heroku (currently $0) People costs - 40 hrs * $65/hr = $10k/mo	30-day free trial then $49/yr

Break-Even Point: 2,000 customers

Lean Canvas is adapted from The Business Model Canvas (http://www.businessmodelgeneration.com) and is licensed under the Creative Commons Attribution-Share Alike 3.0 Un-ported License.

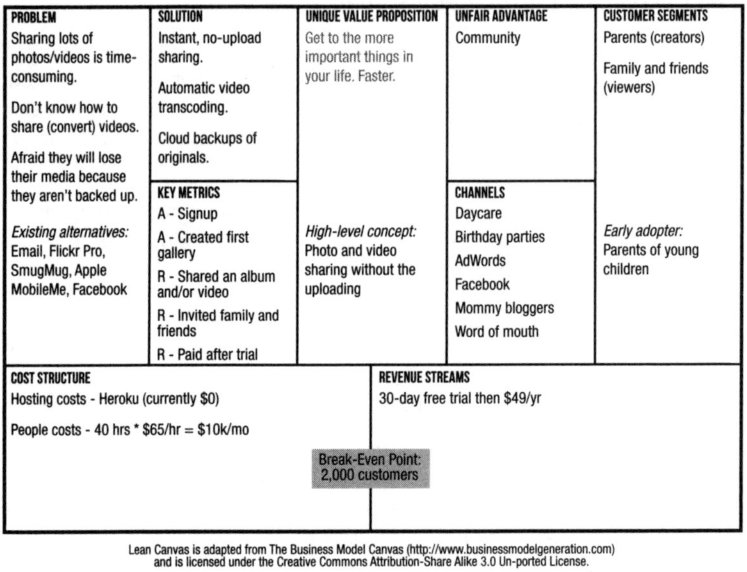

Figure 12-5. *Updated Parents Lean Canvas*

What's next?

Start testing other channels to drive traffic to a much wider audience.

Don't Be a Feature Pusher

In a great market, a market with lots of real potential customers,
the market pulls the product out of the startup.

—*Marc Andreessen, "The Pmarca Guide to Startups"*

Features Must Be Pulled, Not Pushed

Earlier, I advocated implementing a Continuous Deployment system. While Continuous Deployment helps you streamline your product development process for speed, you have to be wary of simply cranking out more features faster.

When you launch your product, lots of things can and will go wrong. Sure enough, feature requests will also start pouring in. The common tendency is to build more, but that is seldom the answer.

Here's why:

More features dilute your unique value proposition (UVP).

You have taken great effort to keep your minimum value proposition (MVP) as small and focused as possible. Don't dilute your UVP with unnecessary distractions.

Simple products are simple to understand.

Don't give up on your MVP too early.

Building great software is hard. While you have painstakingly tested problems worth solving, you have only tested a semblance of the solution. Give your MVP a chance. First troubleshoot and resolve issues with existing features before chasing new features.

Put down the compiler until you learn why they're not buying.
—*Jason Cohen, A Smart Bear blog*

Features always have hidden costs.

More features mean more tests, more screenshots, more videos, more coordination, more complexity, and more distractions.

Start With No.

—*37signals,* Getting Real

You still don't know what customers really want.

Treat your future feature ideas like experiments. Keep them on your feature backlog for now. I'll cover how you prioritize, build, and validate new features shortly.

Feature creep can become an addiction.

—*Ben Yoskovitz,* Instigator *blog*

Implement an 80/20 Rule

A good rule of thumb for prioritizing focus is to implement an 80/20 Rule (see Figure 13-1).

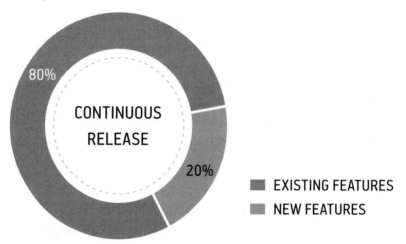

Figure 13-1. *80/20 Rule*

Most of your time immediately after launch should be spent measuring and improving existing features versus chasing after shiny new features.

But even with this breakdown, it's possible to keep cranking out improvements that have zero impact.

The next section helps with that.

Constrain Your Features Pipeline

A good practice for keeping your features pipeline in check is to limit the number of features that can be concurrently worked on *and* only work on new features after you've validated that the features you just deployed had a positive or negative impact (i.e., yielded learning).

A great way to do this is to use a Kanban[1] board (or visual board).

A Kanban board is to feature tracking as a Conversion Dashboard is to metrics tracking. Both let you focus on the macro.

Figure 13-2 shows a very basic Kanban board, with three buckets.

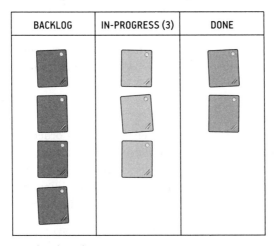

Figure 13-2. *Basic Kanban board*

The general idea is that features start on the lefthand side and move through stages of product and customer development before they are considered "Done."

Here is a high-level overview of the three basic process steps shown in Figure 13-2.

1. Backlog

   All potential features start life in the Backlog bucket. They get in there in one of the following ways:

   – Existing feature improvements (e.g., refined signup flow)

   – Customer feature requests

   – Your feature requests (e.g., the nice-to-haves you deferred earlier)

---

1 Kanban is a scheduling system designed by Taiichi Ohno, father of the Toyota Production System, that tells you what to produce, when to produce, and how much to produce. (Source: *http://en.wikipedia.org/wiki/Kanban*).

Before going further, it is important to distinguish between minimal marketable features (MMFs) and smaller features/bug fixes. MMF was first defined in the book *Software by Numbers* by Mark Denne and Jane Cleland-Huang (Prentice Hall) as the *smallest portion of work that provides value to customers.*

By "feature," I always mean an MMF. A good test for an MMF is to ask yourself if you'd announce it to your customers in a blog post or newsletter. If it's too tiny to mention, it's not an MMF.

An MMF is typically made up of smaller work items (tasks) that, if you are implementing Continuous Deployment, define your small batches. Smaller features and bug fixes typically fit within a work item or small batch.

I only track MMFs on a Kanban board and use a lighter-weight task board tool (like Pivotal Tracker) to track smaller features, bug fixes, and work items.

2. In-Progress

The Backlog queue is usually kept in priority order based on the current goals (focus) of your product. This makes it easy to simply pick the top feature in the list and begin work. The In-Progress step is, in turn, made up of several substeps, such as building mock-ups, coding, deploying, and so forth. I'll cover these details in Chapter 14.

A key principle of Kanban that works to constrain the work queue involves setting limits on the number of features that can be in progress at any given time. This allows you to maximize throughput while minimizing waste. For the technically inclined, Donald Reinertsen's book, *The Principles of Product Development Flow* (Celeritas Publishing), covers why this is so in great detail.

I recommend starting with a work-in-progress limit equal to the number of founders/team members and adjusting later if you need to. So, if you have three founders, only three features can be worked on at any given time.

3. Done

When the feature is done, it's moved into the "Done" bucket. The "Done" state is somewhat arbitrary, and different software development teams use "Done" to mean anything from "Code Complete" to "Tested" to "Deployed."

In a Lean Startup, however, a feature is only "Done" when it *provides validated learning from customers* (see Figure 13-3).

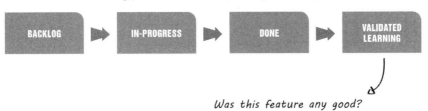

Was this feature any good?

Figure 13-3. *Validated learning stage*

For this reason, Eric Ries suggests either defining "Done" to include validated learning or adding a fourth state for validated learning. As we'll see a little later, I do a bit of both using a two-phase validation—first qualitatively, then quantitatively.

Defining "Done" this way further constrains your feature pipeline and prevents you from working on any new features unless you can prove that the current features just deployed provided validated learning.

Process Feature Requests

In this section, I'll outline a Getting Things Done (GTD) style workflow for how to process new work requests that will inevitably come up (see Figure 13-4).

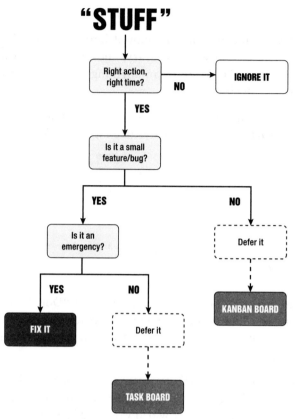

Figure 13-4. *Feature workflow*

The first determination involves checking the request against your product's immediate needs and priorities: is it "Right action, right time?" So, for instance, if you have serious problems with your signup flow, all other downstream requests should take a backseat to that.

After that, you need to consider whether this is a small feature/bug fix or a larger MMF.

If this is a small work item and something that is needed immediately, fix it right away (i.e., code-test-deploy using your Continuous Deployment process). Otherwise, add it to your task board's Backlog bucket. I recommend also keeping the task board Backlog in priority order. That way, anyone on the team can simply pull off a small work item and push it all the way through deployment when she has some idle time.

If this is a larger MMF, it goes on your Kanban board's Backlog bucket. Next, I'll cover how you prioritize and work on these features.

CHAPTER 13

The Feature Lifecycle

The iteration meta-pattern we have been using to define, build, and validate your MVP also applies to MMFs.

In this section, I'll outline a feature lifecycle built on this meta-pattern and implemented using a Kanban board.

How to Track Features on a Kanban Board

Before I get into the specifics of the process steps, I'd like to highlight some general aspects of the Kanban board first (see Figure 13-5).

Goals: **Achieve 60% Activation Rate**

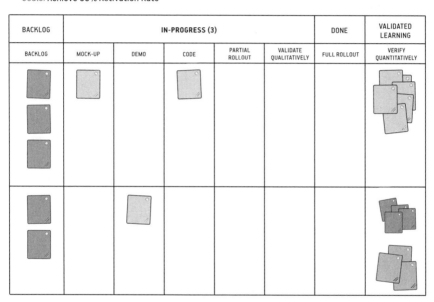

Figure 13-5. *Feature lifecycle*

Goals

> It is a good idea to list your immediate goals and priorities (focus) at the top of your Kanban board. This helps keep everyone on the same page when prioritizing your backlog.

Work-in-progress limits

> The work-in-progress limit is shown in the top header row. It is typical in larger teams to also set limits on each substate (mock-up, demo, code, etc.), but that is overkill at this stage since most startup teams are small.

Buffer lanes

Each process step is divided into two parts. The top section is used for features currently "under work," while the bottom section (also called the buffer) is used to hold features that have been "completed" and are waiting to be picked up for the next process step.

Features that can be killed at any stage

Multiple customer validation stages are built in to the feature lifecycle. If a feature fails validation, either it can be moved back to the previous stage to be reworked or it can be killed. Features slated to be killed are marked in red.

Continuous Deployment

I assume you are following a Continuous Deployment process and group the Commit-Test-Deploy-Monitor cycle simply under Code.

—— **NOTE** ————————————————————————————————————

Even though I am using software in this example, Code could just as easily be replaced with the appropriate Build phase of your product.

Two-phase validation

Because quantitative verification can take a while, I only use qualitative testing to declare a feature as "Done." This releases the work-in-progress lock on that feature so that other features can be worked on while more data is collected.

The Process Steps Explained

Now I'll describe the full feature lifecycle through the process steps.

Understand problem:

1. Backlog

We finished Chapter 12 with a simple workflow for quickly vetting feature requests for your backlog. These are placed in the top part of the Backlog column since they aren't started yet. Because you have a finite work-in-progress limit, you need to carefully prioritize your backlog queue against your product's immediate goals.

Once you have identified a feature, the first step is to test to see if the *problem is worth solving*. If you can't justify building the feature, kill it immediately.

a. Customer-pulled requests

If the feature is a customer-pulled request, arrange a call or meeting with the customer. Even though the customer might be asking for a specific solution, get to the root of the problem. Try to talk the customer out of wanting the feature. Have the customer sell you on why you should add the feature.

At the end of the call, you should be able to assess whether this is a nice-to-have or a must-have problem, whether it is worth solving, and which macro it will affect.

b. Internal requests

If the feature was generated internally, review the same criteria as shown earlier with other team members, and similarly get to an *"Is this worth solving?"* determination for this feature.

Define solution:

1. Mock-up

Once you have a feature worth building, build a mock-up using the same approach outlined in Chapter 8. Start with paper sketches, but quickly get to HTML/CSS views that are ideally accessible from within your application.

2. Demo

With the mock-up ready, conduct an interview similar in structure to the Solution interview that tests your solution with customers. Iterate as needed on the mock-up until you have a strong signal to move forward.

3. Code

With the mock-up validated, you can now start to build the functionality behind the feature. It will most likely make sense to break the feature into a number of smaller work items that you can track using your task board and deploy incrementally using your Continuous Deployment system.

Validate qualitatively:

1. Partial rollout

   Once the feature is coded and ready for use, partially deploy it to just a few customers first.

2. Validate qualitatively

   Conduct usability interviews similar to the MVP interview. Iterate as needed to correct issues.

Verify quantitatively:

1. Full rollout

   You are ready to do a full rollout. Once your feature is rolled out, it is marked "Done," and the lock of the work-in-progress limit is released. This allows you to start working on the next feature in the backlog queue.

2. Verify quantitatively

   With the feature fully live, you should now be able to compare your conversion cohorts for the week the feature went live against the previous week to verify the expected macro impact.

   Depending on the type of feature, you might additionally need to set up a split-test. Split-testing is a matter of judgment at this stage.

   The more concurrent split-tests you have going, the longer the verification time window. Long-running experiments can also start interfering with other experiments and complicate your cohorts. For these reasons, it is best to use your judgment to decide when to split-test and when not to.

   Here are some guidelines:

   - I generally don't split-test a brand-new feature because you can compare against older cohorts that didn't have this feature.
   - I don't split-test experiments that get very strong signals during qualitative testing.
   - I do recommend split-testing experiments that got a medium to strong signal during qualitative testing and those that test improvements or alternate flows.

CHAPTER 14

Measure Product/Market Fit

The first step is to define a metric to measure product/market fit. Once you have that, you can systematically iterate toward achieving it.

What Is Product/Market Fit?

Even though Marc Andreessen did not coin the term *product/market fit*,[1] his blog post on the topic remains one of the most popular descriptions of what product/market fit feels like:

> *Product/Market fit means being in a good market with a product that can satisfy that market.*
>
> *You can always feel when product/market fit isn't happening. The customers aren't quite getting value out of the product, word of mouth isn't spreading, usage isn't growing that fast, press reviews are kind of "blah," the sales cycle takes too long, and lots of deals never close.*
>
> *And you can always feel product/market fit when it's happening. The customers are buying the product just as fast as you can make it—or usage is growing just as fast as you can add more servers. Money from customers is piling up in your company checking account. You're hiring sales and customer support staff as fast as you can. Reporters are calling because they've heard about your hot new thing and they want to talk to you about it.*
>
> —*Marc Andreessen, "The Pmarca Guide to Startups"*

---

1   The term *product/market fit* was coined by Andy Rachleff, who cofounded the VC firm Benchmark Capital.

Unfortunately, Marc ended that post with more questions than answers and didn't offer any guidance on how to achieve or measure product/market fit. Sean Ellis makes the concept less abstract by offering a metric for determining early traction that is a prerequisite to achieving product/market fit. I will cover this next.

The Sean Ellis Test

Sean Ellis ran a consulting company, 12in6, which specialized in helping startups during their growth transition stage. As a condition to taking on a client, he conducted a qualitative survey across a sampling of the company's users to determine if the company's product had early traction, which was a good indicator that the company was on the right track.

The key question on the survey was:

How would you feel if you could no longer use [product]?

1. Very disappointed

2. Somewhat disappointed

3. Not disappointed (it isn't really that useful)

4. N/A – I no longer use [product]

If you find that over 40% of your users are saying that they would be "very disappointed" without your product, there is a great chance you can build sustainable, scalable customer acquisition growth on this "must have" product. This 40% benchmark was determined by comparing results across hundreds of startups. Those that were above 40% are generally able to sustainably scale the businesses; those significantly below 40% always seem to struggle. [2]

I feel the exact wording of the question could use some slight tweaking depending on your target market. For example, in a B2B/enterprise context, posturing to take away a product may not sit well with your early customers who are investing time in your product. Aside from that, the basic premise of the test is sound. It attempts to measure your product's resonance with users.

The bigger challenge, though, with implementing Sean's test, is the same one I outlined earlier with customer surveys:

Surveys are more effective at verification than learning.

---

2   *http://startup-marketing.com/using-survey-io/*

In this case, while Sean's test can help *determine if* you have early traction, it doesn't help you *achieve it*.

Additionally, for the results to be statistically significant, you need to have a large enough sample size, account for customer segmentation, and consider user motivation. For these reasons, the test is best administered when you are close to product/market fit (which is also what Sean recommends).

So, what do you do until then? How do you steer your product toward product/market fit?

The answer lies within your conversion dashboard. In the next section, I'll outline another approach to measuring your product's early resonance with users using two key metrics from your customer lifecycle—activation and retention, which together make up your value metrics.

Focus on the "Right" Macro

> *Build something people want.*
>
> —*Paul Graham*

Achieving product/market fit or traction can fundamentally be reduced to building something people want or, in other words, delivering on your UVP. Some products are designed to capture one-time value—for example, wedding photographers, divorce attorneys, books, DVDs, and so on. Other products are designed to capture recurring value through repeated use—for example, Software as a Service products, social networking services, restaurants, magazines, and so on.

The first is primarily driven by the experience of the service, which can be effectively measured using the activation metric. The second also relies on a good first experience (so good activation is still important), but success is driven through repeat usage—making *retention* the more indicative measure of "building something people want" (see Figure 14-1).

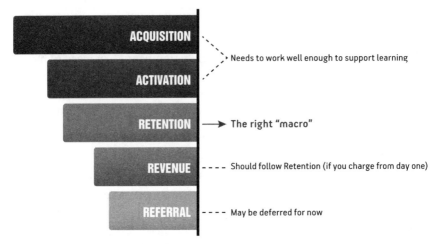

Figure 14-1. *Focusing on the right macro*

The argument can be made that repeated use of a product over a long enough period should correlate closely enough to the responses of Sean's "very disappointed" survey question. This makes it possible to apply the same 40% threshold to determining early traction.[3]

You have early traction when you are retaining 40% of your activated users, month after month.

What About Revenue?

While I believe pricing is part of the product and advocate charging from day one, revenue is only the first form of validation and, when used just by itself, could be a false positive as a product/market fit test. I've experienced numerous cases with my products where customers kept paying for a product they did not use (not even sporadically). Sometimes this was because someone else was paying (their company, for instance) or they simply forgot to cancel the product.

Other times, I've seen startups get distracted by chasing the wrong type of revenue—for example, doing one-time licensing/custom development deals.

While revenue is the first form of validation, retention is the ultimate form of validation.

Furthermore, if you offer a one-time product, charge appropriately, *and* have good activation, revenue will take care of itself. Similarly, if you offer a subscription service and charge from day one *and* you have good retention, revenue will take care of itself.

---

3   I consulted Sean Ellis on this and he agreed.

Have You Built Something People Want?

In this section, I'll summarize the process of iterating toward early traction and determining when you have achieved it:

1. Review your conversion dashboard results weekly.

   Set a time every Monday to review your weekly conversion dashboard with the entire team. Identify the leakiest buckets you need to fix first.

2. Prioritize your goals and features backlog.

   Review your features backlog to prioritize new and existing feature improvements.

3. Formulate bold hypotheses.

   At this stage, avoid micro-optimization experiments. Instead, come up with bold hypotheses, but build the smallest thing possible to test them.

4. Add/kill features.

   Review features throughout the feature lifecycle to ensure that they have a positive impact. Otherwise, rework or kill them.

5. Monitor your value metrics.

   Review your retention cohorts. Your goal is to see steady upward movement in these numbers. Otherwise, you're simply spinning your wheels.

6. Run the Sean Ellis Test.

   Once your retention numbers approach 40%, consider running the Sean Ellis Test.

What Are the Early Traction Exit Criteria?

You are done when you can:

- Retain 40% of your users
- Pass the Sean Ellis Test

What About the Market in Product/Market Fit?

By that I mean things like churn, viral coefficient, cost of customer acquisition, lifetime value—things that make your business model scalable.

Focusing on scaling your business before you can demonstrate early traction is a form of waste.

Once you can demonstrate early traction, your focus should shift toward achieving sustainable growth.

Start by Identifying Your Key Engine of Growth

The engine of growth is the mechanism that startups use to achieve sustainable growth.

> —Eric Ries, The Lean Startup *(Crown Business)*

In his book, Eric Ries describes the three engines of growth as follows:

Sticky: high retention

A product that uses the sticky engine of growth relies on having a high customer retention rate (or a low churn rate). Examples: telephone/cable service providers, Software-as-a-Service (SaaS) products.

Churn rate is the fraction of customers who leave or fail to remain engaged with a product after a given time period.

Growth here is driven by keeping Customer Acquisition Rate > Churn Rate.

Viral: high referral

A product that uses the viral engine of growth relies on having a high customer-to-customer referral rate (or a high viral coefficient), which is often a built-in side effect of using the product. Examples: online social networks like Facebook and Twitter.

Viral coefficient measures the number of converted referrals per customer.

Growth here is driven by keeping the Viral Coefficient > 1 (i.e., each user brings in at least one other user).

Paid: high margins

A product that uses the paid engine of growth relies on reinvesting a portion of customer revenues (lifetime value or LTV) toward customer acquisition activities like buying advertising or hiring sales people.

Growth here is driven by keeping customer lifetime value (LTV) > cost of customer acquisition (COCA).

A good rule of thumb by way of David Skok, Matrix Partners, is to keep LTV > 3 * COCA.

So which one do you pick?

While some or all of these may apply to your product, it's important to focus on a single engine first that has the most potential for impact given your specific product's path to customers (channels).

What's stopping your business from growing 10x?

> —David Skok

It is typical for the right selection to be nonobvious, as many products exhibit some elements of all three, and the "right" engine of growth can also change over time.

Here are some general guidelines to make the selection process easier:

1. Start with validating your value metrics.

   Every product has to start by demonstrating and delivering a basic value proposition to customers.

2. Understand how customers behave with your product.

   Study your baseline customer lifecycle to identify any particular usage patterns:

   - If you have implicit virality built into your product—that is, users repeatedly bring in other users as a natural side effect of using your service (e.g., Facebook and Twitter)—you might consider investing in a viral engine of growth. Often, that also drives the lowering of signup friction, such as making the service free to maximize user growth.

   - If you have a recurring use model—for example, a Software as a Service product—it might be worthwhile to invest your effort initially to drive up the lifetime value of your customers by reducing your churn rate. At some point, you will hit a ceiling of diminishing returns, which might be your cue to switch to another engine of growth, like paid. In these types of products, even though you might have some referrals, the referrals do not repeat beyond one or two degrees (i.e., the viral coefficient is less than 1).

   - If you have a one-time-use product that isn't also viral, such as the wedding photographer and divorce attorney examples, your only bet is to invest in the paid engine of growth. Again, your product might exhibit word-of-mouth referrals, and you may even have repeat customers, but neither of these are key to driving sustainable growth.

3. Pick an engine to tune.

   Once you've selected your key engine of growth, put a stake in the ground: Declare the key metric and improvement you want to achieve. Then, align your next set of experiments toward that goal.

CloudFire: Pivot, Persevere, or Reset

By the end of the preceding stage, we had signed up a number of moms who helped us further refine the minimum viable product (MVP). A fair percentage of them made it to the end of the customer lifecycle, resulting in paid subscribers and favorable customer testimonials.

However, as we opened CloudFire to a larger audience, we faced new challenges with scaling to more customers. While we were building a product targeted at busy first-time moms, the very fact that they were so busy (dealing with a significant life-changing event) was getting in the way of getting the right level of attention (engine of growth challenge). There had been several early warning signs, in the form of last-minute scheduling cancellations and multiple follow-ups, that we had failed to pick up on.

In parallel, we had also been testing CloudFire for the photographers market (using a separately branded "pro website") and narrowed in on wedding photographers as early adopters. Unlike moms, their livelihood depended on sharing and selling this content. As a result, they were much more motivated to both use and pay more for CloudFire. But there was an even more unplanned connection between these two customer segments.

Wedding photographers were in the ideal position to sell CloudFire to newlyweds who may eventually use the service for other significant "life events," like having a baby—thereby increasing the lifetime value of the service.

Wedding photographers were motivated to act as channel partners because CloudFire allowed them to differentiate their offering and potentially benefit from branding and search engine optimization (SEO) benefits we were building into the product.

While all this sounded promising, there was a *problem*. I had founded this company around a technical vision and a prototypical customer that looked more like me than a mom or wedding photographer. While I had great passion for the technology behind the solution, I found myself with little passion for the customers or their problems.

Only having passion for the solution is a problem.

Looking back, I can see how this happened. My entrepreneurial journey so far can be described in three stages:

1. Lure of Creative Addiction: Entrepreneurs Are Artists

> *We built it and we didn't expect it to be a company, we were just building this because we thought it was awesome.*
>
> —Mark Zuckerberg

—continued—

Like many entrepreneurs, I was initially driven by an inexplicable need to "create"—to build something unique that potentially changes the world.

I started my company back in 2002, building a private social networking app called 6Degrees. Little did I know that only months later Friendster would launch, followed by dozens of other social networking sites. That didn't stop us, because we were taking a different approach (built on privacy and decentralization). Competition felt like validation and gave us permission to keep "creating" more. Privacy and social networking back in 2002 didn't go together.

Lesson 1: Being different is good only if that difference matters.

2. Startup As Survival: Artists Need to Eat, Too

   Fairly early on, you have to figure out how you are going to set up enough of a runway to afford the "starting-up dip."

   Bootstrapping wasn't my first choice. I had just been part of a nine-digit startup exit (largely owned by the founders), so I set up a meeting with the founders. To my surprise, while they liked the concept, they were unwilling to fund its development. This was the first of many lessons to come on understanding startup risks and the true job of an entrepreneur. I didn't completely understand this one at the time.

   Capital was really tight back in 2002 (especially in Texas), but I was determined to move forward. I eventually got a "lucky break" from an entrepreneur in Norway who found me through a blog post and funded the development of the platform I was building in exchange for a discounted licensing deal.

   > The amount of serendipity that will occur in your life, your Luck Surface Area, is directly proportional to the degree to which you do something you're passionate about combined with the total number of people to whom this is effectively communicated.
   > —Jason Roberts, "How to Increase Your Luck Surface Area"

   Even back then, I placed a premium on my time. I made a deal with my wife that I would use money as the barometer for success—building enough of a runway so that I could afford my creative addiction was the prize here.

   Strangely enough, I never missed a single paycheck for seven years straight and got really good at survival, which became a new reason for being. I gradually became less interested in learning how to build complex products and more interested in learning how to build successful products.

   Up until now, I had built products in stealth, attempted building a platform, dabbled with open sourcing, practiced "release early, release often," embraced "less is more," and even tried "more is more." This is also when I ran into Customer Development, and from this I followed the trail to Lean Startups, which completely changed my approach to vetting and building products.

—continued—

With CloudFire, while I succeeded in discovering viable "customer problems" to solve and even got pretty far in terms of validating the business model (with positive cash flow), something was grossly missing: *passion for customers and their problems.*

I had unknowingly tweaked my founding vision along the way from being problem-based—"connecting everyone on this planet"—to being solution-based—"a peer-to-web framework that blurs the boundaries between the desktop and the Web." I had become a company with a "solution looking for a problem" and the viable customers and markets I found were unexpected.

Lesson 2: Making money is the first form of validation, but that may not be enough.

3. Curse of Legacy: Artists Need to Constantly Reinvent Themselves

   People form a startup for several reasons, many of which lead to successful businesses (and/or exits). However, I had reached a stage where I was looking for something more: purpose.

   I was forced to confront my problem–passion disconnect and saw two options. I could hire in the missing passion for these segments, or I could sell the company. Legacy can be an advantage or a constraining disadvantage, and this wasn't an easy decision to make.

   In the past two years, I had stumbled into new sets of problems, ones that struck a chord on many levels. I had set up my blog as a way to hold myself publicly accountable, but along the way I got swept into the world of Lean Startups and joined in on the conversation. I was positively surprised by the reaction and encouragement I received. I reluctantly started writing this book and even more uncomfortably started running workshops.

   When I saw enough dots connecting, I decided to hit the reset button. I called up my first customer from Norway (Sverre Fjeldheim) and within two weeks we had a deal for a sale. After a short period of company transition, I started laying the groundwork for a new company: Spark59.

   Lesson 3: Startups can consume years of your life, so pick a problem worth solving.

A good hack for finding a problem worth solving (codified with the help of Patrick Smith) is immersing yourself completely in a vertical (any vertical) you are passionate about and surrounding yourself with other passionate people. People inevitably have problems, and you (the entrepreneur) are wired to look for solutions.

Summary

Figure 14-2 captures the workflow we've followed throughout this book.

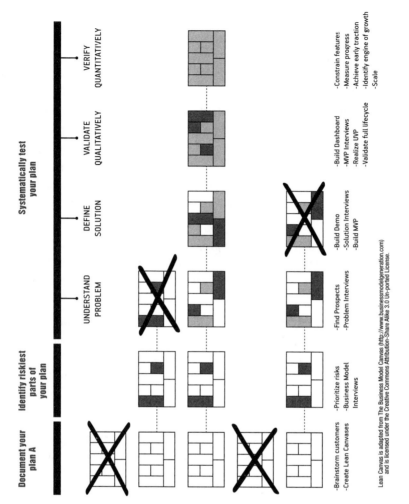

Figure 14-2. *The Running Lean methodology*

While this pattern applies to a wide range of products, I am frequently asked how one might adapt it to two models in particular: a network effects product and a multisided (marketplace) product.

Design Pattern for a Network Effects Product

A network effects product is a product whose value depends on the number of people using it. The telephone is the classic example, and online services like Twitter and Facebook also operate under this model.

The same meta-pattern we've covered so far can also be applied to these types of products, with a few additional considerations:

Attention is a convertible asset.

As the value of the product grows with the number of users, there is "some" convertible formula for valuing the number of active users as an asset in lieu of "actual revenue" on the Revenue Streams section in the canvas.

This formula can be hard to pin down, but current advertising rates and/or valuations of similarly modeled products may be a place to start.

One challenge with these types of products is that the product typically has to pass a certain tipping point for this valuation to kick in. Up until then, the startup has to find a way to survive through very uncertain times.

Twitter started as a "fun" side-project likened to ice-cream, while Ev Williams was working on his main company, Odeo, which had raised millions of dollars from investors.

—Source: New York Times

When Zuckerberg moved out to Silicon Valley in his sophomore summer, he thought that maybe one day he and his team would develop a startup, but didn't think Facebook was that startup.

—Source: TechCrunch

Retention is still king.

The first significant milestone still centers around building something people want as measured by repeated usage or engagement (value metrics). For more on this, see the sidebar, "Validate Value Before Growth: Facebook."

The engine of growth is viral.

Once your value metrics are validated at a micro scale, you need to race toward your critical network tipping point using the viral engine of growth. Once there, you can look to validate your attention currency through means such as advertising (e.g., Facebook), premium memberships (e.g., LinkedIn), or something else.

—————— **NOTE** ———————————————————————————

While one could argue that a network effects product with advertising is a form of a multisided (marketplace) model, I tend to reserve that label for a service where both sides actively work together to transact business. That is the topic of the next section.

——

Validate Value Before Growth: Facebook

Facebook wasn't the first social network, but it has grown to become the largest. Something its founders did very differently was seeding their product in a preexisting offline social network, the Harvard University campus. Rather than scaling the service to everyone, they methodically validated their value assumptions first, from one college campus to another, and ended up with both a high-value and a high-growth product.

Design Pattern for a Multisided (Marketplace) Product

A multisided product is a product that connects buyers and sellers and provides value by reducing transaction friction. Classic examples here are eBay, Expedia, and Priceline.

For some reason, I find a lot of entrepreneurs are drawn to this model. It's probably because this model appears to be the easiest to monetize. After all, the purpose of a marketplace is to transact business. But these marketplaces can be notoriously difficult to establish for the commonly cited "chicken and egg problem":

Buyers aren't interested because you lack enough sellers, and vice versa.

Here are some thoughts on how to navigate this model:

Create canvases for both sides.

> In a way, you are building two business models in one. You have to understand who the sellers are, how you'll reach them, and what unique value you'll provide them. Then do the same for the buyers. Creating separate canvases for each is a great way to document these assumptions.

Validate value in a prototypical early adopter submarketplace.

> As with the network effects product, your first job is to demonstrate value at a micro scale. Rather than creating a new or large marketplace, identify a prototypical preexisting "early adopter" marketplace where both the motivation and the friction for transacting business is currently high.

> For instance, if you're building a marketplace that connects adventure tour operators with service providers, home in on a specific activity like rock climbing in your local area where you have direct access to both sides. Similarly, if you're looking to facilitate selling multiple categories of products, pick a single niche category first.

Run separate Problem and Solution interviews to validate your assumptions around pain level and motivations of both buyers and sellers. Get commitments, build an MVP, and start connecting buyers with sellers. For an example of this, see the sidebar, "Reduce Marketplace Friction at a Micro Scale First: Airbnb."

Don't automate match making.

Matching buyers and sellers is a hard problem. Consider using a "Concierge MVP" model (like the Food on the Table case study from Chapter 5) to keep the quality level high while you learn what to automate. The sidebar "Learn Manually Before Automating: AngelList" provides another example of this.

Identify the right engine of growth for each side.

You can probably leverage early testimonials to enter neighboring marketplaces. But be wary of recognizing that you may need to simultaneously tune two separate engines of growth for each side of the marketplace.

Reduce Marketplace Friction at a Micro Scale First: Airbnb

Airbnb is an online service that matches people seeking vacation rentals and other short-term accommodations with people in those cities with rooms to rent. As of this writing, Airbnb carries listings from more than 16,000 cities in 186 countries. But Airbnb didn't get this far without a lot of long, hard learning. In their first experiment, which launched the product, the founders offered their place for rent during a sold-out, prominent design conference. They ran two additional experiments—one during SXSW in Austin, Texas, and the other during the Democratic National Convention in Denver—all the while consulting on the side. They joined the Y Combinator program shortly after, where they focused on the product full-time and systematically rolled it out from city to city.

Learn Manually Before Automating: AngelList

When AngelList first launched, founders Nivi and Naval relentlessly spent a lot of their personal time vetting and coaching companies most likely to be funded, which they then manually paired with high-quality investors through email introductions. This ensured a high quality of deal flow evidenced by favorable testimonials from both investors and entrepreneurs that helped fuel their growth. It also allowed them to learn parts of the "manual process" that would most benefit from automation that they then built in to their online solution.

CHAPTER 15

Conclusion

Congratulations! We're done.

What's Next?

> *I believe that the life of any startup can be divided into two parts: before product/market fit (call this "BPMF") and after product/market fit ("APMF").*
>
> —*Marc Andreessen, "The Pmarca Guide to Startups"*

Life After Product/Market Fit

Getting to product/market fit is the first significant milestone of a startup. At this stage, some level of success is almost guaranteed and your focus can now shift from learning to scaling (see Figure 15-1).

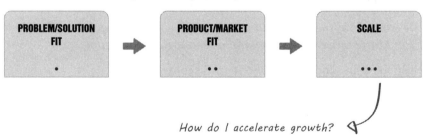

Figure 15-1. *After product/market fit*

Along with continually tuning and resetting your engine of growth to meet customer adoption challenges as you attempt to "cross the chasm" between early adopters and mainstream customers,[1] you will inevitably also be faced with new challenges as you grow your company.

Every process works well until you add people.

The key is to build a continuous learning culture of experimenters versus specialists, where it's everyone's job to be accountable toward creating and capturing customer value.

> *The Toyota style is not to create results by working hard. It is a system that says there is no limit to people's creativity. People don't go to Toyota to "work," they go there to "think."*
>
> —*Taiichi Ohno*

Did I Keep My Promise?

I started this book stating that no methodology can guarantee success, but I promised a repeatable, actionable process for building products, *one that raises your odds for success by helping you identify your success metrics and measure progress against those metrics.*

I hope I delivered on that promise.

There is no better time than the present to start up, and the ideas in this book will help you do just that. In fact, you'll find that once you internalize the core principles presented here, you'll see applications for them all over the place.

Keep In Touch

A book, like large software, is never finished—only released.

This book is only the beginning. I continue to share my learning on my blog at *http://ashmaurya.com* and periodically teach workshops.

For even more tactical techniques, consider subscribing to my *Running Lean Mastery* newsletter: *http://blog.runningleanhq.com/mastery/.*

Drop me a line anytime at *ash@spark59.com.*

Twitter: @ashmaurya

Skype: ashmaurya

Thanks for reading, and here's to your success!

---

1 Geoffrey Moore describes this chasm in his book, *Crossing the Chasm: Marketing and Selling High-Tech Products to Mainstream Customers* (HarperBusiness).

Resources

Books

- *The Lean Startup* by Eric Ries (Crown Business)
- *The Four Steps to the Epiphany* by Steve Blank (*http://www.cafepress.com/kandsranch*)
- *Business Model Generation* by Alex Osterwalder (Wiley)
- *The Entrepreneur's Guide to Customer Development* by Brant Cooper and Patrick Vlaskovits (Cooper-Vlaskovits)
- *Positioning: The Battle for Your Mind* by Jack Trout and Al Ries (Warner Books)
- *Don't Just Roll the Dice* by Neil Davidson (Red Gate Books)
- *Rocket Surgery Made Easy* by Steve Krug (New Riders Press)
- *Inbound Marketing* by Dharmesh Shah and Brian Halligan (Wiley)
- *The Principles of Product Development Flow* by Donald Reinertsen (Celeritas Publishing)
- *Lean Software Development: An Agile Toolkit* by Mary Poppendieck and Tom Poppendieck (Addison-Wesley Professional)
- *Toyota Production System* by Taiichi Ohno (Productivity Press)

Blogs

- Eric Ries, "Startup Lessons Learned" (*http://startuplessonslearned.com*)
- Steve Blank (*http://steveblank.com*)
- Jason Cohen, "A Smart Bear" (*http://blog.asmartbear.com*)
- Venture Hacks (*http://venturehacks.com*)
- Sean Ellis, "Startup Marketing" (*http://startup-marketing.com*)
- Dharmesh Shah, "OnStartups" (*http://onstartups.com*)
- David Skok, "For Entrepreneurs" (*http://www.forentrepreneurs.com*)
- Ben Yoskovitz, "instigator blog" (*http://www.instigatorblog.com*)

Tools

- Lean Canvas: business model validation software (*http://leancanvas.com*)
- USERcycle: customer lifecycle management software (*http://usercycle.com*)
- User Testing: online usability testing (*http://usertesting.com*)
- KISSmetrics: actionable web analytics software (*http://kissmetrics.com*)
- Mixpanel: real-time event tracking (*http://mixpanel.com*)
- SnapEngage: online customer feedback tool (*http://snapengage.com*)
- Heroku: Ruby Platform-as-a-Service infrastructure (*http://heroku.com*)

Bonus Material

How to Build a Low-Burn Startup

I've bootstrapped my company for the past seven years and learned a lot about bootstrapping from Bijoy Goswami, founder of Bootstrap Austin. Bijoy doesn't limit the definition of bootstrapping to the more commonly held one about *building a company without external funding*, but rather views bootstrapping as a philosophy summarized as *"Right action, right time."*

This mantra applies just as well to Lean Startups as it does to bootstrapped startups:

At every stage of the startup, there are a set of actions that are "right" for the startup, in that they maximize return on time, money, and effort. A lean/bootstrapped entrepreneur ignores all else.

While bootstrapping and Lean Startup techniques are not just limited to funding, funding is one of the first problems entrepreneurs tackle, which can lead to waste.

Why Premature Fundraising Is a Form of Waste

There are several reasons why premature funding can lead to waste:

Getting funded is not validation.

Seed stage investors are just as bad at guessing what products will succeed as you are. Without any product validation to rely on, they hedge their bets against your team's track record and storytelling ability. So, while getting funded at this stage is a testament to your team-building and pitching skills, it isn't product validation.

Without validation, you have no leverage.

More important, without validation, you don't have product/market credibility, which typically comes at a price—reflected in lower valuations and investor-favored term sheets.

Investors measure progress differently.

While validated learning is the measure of progress in a Lean Startup, most investors measure progress through growth. Reconciling the two during the early stages of a startup (when the hockey stick is largely flat) can be both challenging and distracting.

Getting funded always takes longer than you think.

Time is more valuable than money. Would you rather spend months pitching investors so that you can refine a story based on an untested product, or spend time pitching customers so that you can tell a credible story based on a tested product?

Too much money can actually hurt you.

Money is an accelerant, not a silver bullet. It lets you do more of what you're currently doing, but not necessarily do it better. For instance, more money might tempt you to hire more people and build more features—both of which may lead you off course and slow you down.

Constraints drive innovation, but more important, they force action.

With less money, you are forced to build less, get it out faster, and learn faster.

What about all the advice and connections?

Raising funding is not the only way to get good advice. You can and should start building a diverse board of advisors early. Many are happy just to be asked; others might require a little equity to formalize a relationship.

How do I survive until product/market fit?

While the ideal time to raise external funding is after product/market fit, you might need to raise a smaller round before then, or self-fund. The goal is to get as close to product/market fit as possible.

The biggest reason for bootstrapping first is that it is easier than ever to start a company, or more accurately test to see if you even have a company. You don't need much to start defining, building, and testing a minimum viable product (MVP) toward product/market fit. With the right team (and skill set) in place, you can validate problem/solution fit while keeping your day job, and put an MVP in front of customers soon after that.

Here are some other tips to help you along the way:

Keep your day job.

The first stage, finding problem/solution fit, can really be done part-time with very little burn. It typically has a lot of waiting time built in (e.g., contacting customers, scheduling interviews, collecting results). Until you find a problem worth solving, it really doesn't make sense to quit your day job. The outcome of this stage should be a handful of features.

Build just those features, and nothing else.

While all this can usually be done in your spare time, I highly recommend reviewing your company's moonlighting clause.

> —— **NOTE** ————————————————————————
>
> Disclaimer: I am not a lawyer. You should consult a lawyer before applying this to your particular situation.

Conserve burn rate.

The biggest burn in a software business is people. Hardware is cheap. Rent, don't buy. Don't scale until you have a scaling problem. Don't hire until it hurts.

Charge from day one.

Make a goal of first covering your hardware/hosting costs, and then your people costs.

Sell other related stuff along the way.

It is very tempting to take on unrelated consulting to survive, but it becomes very hard (if not outright impossible) to build a great product in parallel. Instead, look for other related stuff that you can sell along the way. License a piece of your technology, write a book (like this one), teach workshops, get paid to speak, and so on. Not only are these things related to your core business, but many of them also help you build up your online reputation and brand, which pays off over time and could even lead to an unfair advantage.

How to Achieve Flow in a Lean Startup

In a Lean Startup, eliminating waste is a fundamental principle.

> *Waste is any human activity which absorbs resources but creates no value.*
>
> —*James P. Womak and Daniel T. Jones,*
> Lean Thinking *(Free Press)*

Of all resources, there is no resource more valuable than time. Time is more valuable than money. While money can fluctuate up or down, time only moves in one direction.

The Conflicting Pull for Time

Time, like any resource, has multiple pulls. In following customer development, there is a basic pull for activities outside the building versus inside the building. Steve Blank asserts that all the answers lie outside the building and advocates the creation of a cross-functional customer development team *that must include the founders.* What about work that needs to get done inside the building? Who is going to implement the solutions to problems uncovered outside the building?

Eric Ries's answer is to create two teams that feed into each other: a problem team and a solution team. The problem team focuses on customer development, while the solution team focuses on product development.

However, if you are a founder, you need to be on both teams, and this is where the fundamental *scheduling tug-of-war* problem lies.

The problem is further exacerbated if you are a technical founder (like me), because time is utilized very differently when switching from product development to customer development. Paul Graham wrote an excellent essay[1] on the two types of schedules: manager's schedule and maker's schedule.

Managers typically organize their day into one-hour blocks, and spend each hour dealing with a different task. Makers, like programmers and writers, need to organize their day into longer blocks of uninterrupted time. The cost of context switching is low (and expected) in a manager's schedule. It is high (and a productivity killer) in a maker's schedule.

Activities outside the building (customer interviews, usability testing, customer support) tend to be on a manager's schedule, while activities inside the building (design, coding) are usually on a maker's schedule.

---

1 "Maker's Schedule, Manager's Schedule," by Paul Graham (*http://www.paulgraham.com/ makersschedule.html*).

Trying to find an equilibrium point between these two pulls is more art than science, but there is a fundamental concept that must be present to maximize productivity: *flow*.

There are two different definitions to what I mean by flow, and both apply here.

The first comes from psychologist Mihály Csíkszentmihályi, who defines flow as a mental state of operation when you are at your best. When you are *in flow*, you are so totally immersed in an activity that nothing else matters. You lose your self-consciousness and sense of time.

Activities that flow typically have the following attributes:

- They have a clear objective.

- They need your full concentration.

- They lack interruptions and distractions.

- They provide clear and immediate feedback on progress toward the objective.

- They offer a sense of challenge.

While flow can't be triggered at will, you can arrange activities so that they allow for flow, which, coincidently, is also the second definition of flow:

> *When we start thinking about the ways to line up essential steps to get a job done to achieve a steady continuous flow with no wasted energy, batches, or queues, it changes everything including how we collaborate and the tools we devise to get the job done.*
>
> —*Womak and Jones*, Lean Thinking

What follows are specific work hacks I use to allow for flow.

Creating Daily Flow

I generally group my daily activities into three categories: planned maker activities, planned manager activities, and unplanned maker/manager activities.

Work Hack 1: Establish uninterruptible time blocks for maker work.

My planned maker activities are typically coding and writing tasks I've previously identified. Because these activities need an uninterruptible block of time, I schedule these very early in the morning (6:00 a.m.– 8:00 a.m.). I usually schedule this task the night before, and it is the first and only thing I do. I don't check email or Twitter or look at anything else. No one is calling at that hour, so distractions are at a minimum. I find two-hour blocks work best for me.

Work Hack 2: Achieve maker goals as early in the day as possible.

I've tried both staying up late and waking up early, and I prefer the latter as it isn't interrupted by sleep, which allows the day's activities to flow better. I also find that accomplishing something tangible that early in the day sets the tone for the rest of the day.

Depending on the day of the week, I might allocate more two-hour blocks later in the morning or afternoon, but they aren't as intense as the first one and can be interrupted by something more urgent.

Work Hack 3: Schedule manager activities as late in the day as possible.

Planned manager activities, like customer meetings, are easier to schedule because they are clearly time-boxed and calendar-driven. Unless there is an unworkable schedule conflict, I prefer to schedule these for the afternoon so as not to interrupt my morning flow.

Work Hack 4: Always be ready for unplanned activities like customer support.

Unexpected interruptions can surface from anywhere throughout the day—server issues, customer support calls, and so on. You have to be prepared for interruptions, especially from customers. Both server alerts and customer calls (1-800 number) are routed directly to my mobile phone. This is also a good place to apply a Five Whys process to ensure that unexpected incidents don't become recurring incidents (I will discuss this process in more detail shortly).

Creating Weekly Flow

Aside from organizing the day for flow, I also group certain activities of tasks by day of the week:

Work Hack 5: Identify the best days for planned Customer Development.

For instance, Mondays and Fridays are usually bad days for initiating new customer contact, as people are generally either recovering from the weekend or getting ready for it. I plan these types of customer development activities for Tuesday through Thursday.

Work Hack 6: Take advantage of customer downtime.

Since Mondays and Fridays are usually slower from a customer per-spective, I use these days for larger maker tasks, like writing blog posts. My blog posts are usually identified on Friday, outlined over the weekend, written/proofed on Monday, and published on Tuesday.

Work Hack 7: Balance face time with customers.

Not all customer development activities require face time. Beyond the initial customer discovery stage, there is a strong tendency to rely more heavily on asynchronous communication using tools like email, forums, and online usability testing. While all these tools are great for lowering real-time distractions and achieving scale, I find it important to still create opportunities for face time with existing and new customers.

Unscripted conversations are the best way for learning about unscripted problems.

I put our 1-800 number on all pages and encourage customers to pick up the phone versus emailing whenever possible.

Eliminating Software Waste

Building software to specifications is hard enough that, when faced with a startup environment where both problems and solutions are largely unknown, it is optimal to iterate around less code and more learning.

Work Hack 8: Avoid overproduction by making customers pull for features.

Customer pull is another concept from "Lean," and it requires that no product or service be produced until a customer asks for it.

Eighty percent of your effort should be spent toward optimizing existing features versus building new ones.

The whole point of Customer Development is to identify an MVP that resonates with customers, and the whole point of customer validation is to test whether that resonance will scale. If it doesn't, the answer is not adding features, but possibly pivoting and going back to Step 1: customer discovery.

Work Hack 9: Iterate around only three to five actionable metrics.

A few actionable metrics are all you need to identify and prioritize the most critical issues to tackle.

Work Hack 10: Build software to flow.

You might have noticed that I don't have days or tasks identified for building, testing, or releasing software. That is because I follow a continuous deployment process (also popularized by Eric Ries) where software is built, tested, and packaged automatically at the end of every maker task, with no effort on my part other than checking in code. One click, and the code is released to customers.

Manufacturing processes have traditionally been arranged around machine time-breaking tasks into batches and queues. "Lean" challenges this approach and calls for arranging around human time-organizing tasks so that they flow.

Releasing software is not unlike manufacturing of physical products. While it is somewhat easier to continuously deploy web-based software, with a little discipline, desktop-based software also can be built to flow.

How to Set Pricing for a SaaS Product

The initial objective of a startup is learning, not optimization. The strategy I've found that works is *starting with a single "Free Trial" pricing plan.*

Start with a single pricing plan.

Starting with multiple plans that cover everyone under the sun is a form of waste. I've seen startups launch with plan options targeting one-person startups to enterprises composed of more than a thousand people.

Not only does supporting multiple plans require you to write more code to support plan/feature segmentation, but the return on learning is diluted when you attempt to target multiple customer segments all at once. In the example in the preceding paragraph, the business models and tactics vary greatly when selling to startups as opposed to selling to enterprises.

The bigger point here, though, is that when you're starting out, you don't yet have enough information to know how to correctly price or segment the feature set into multiple plans.

Use a "Free Trial" plan.

Time-based trials help time-box your pricing experiments so that you can force a conversion decision, which allows you to learn and iterate faster.

Pick a price to test.

Existing alternatives create "reference points" in the minds of customers that they will use to rank your solution, so it's important to understand and position your price against them.

In the rare case that you are actually solving a brand-new problem or don't have clear reference points (more common in enterprise-based products), you might have to pick a starting price out of thin air and refine from there.

Pricing is all about setting the right perception.
—*Neil Davidson,* Don't Just Roll the Dice *(Red Gate Books)*

Take your costs into account.

The ultimate goal is to find a scalable business model, so it should go without saying that you also need to keep an eye on what it would cost you to deliver your solution and ensure that you have a healthy margin built in.

One rule of thumb for building a successful business (by way of David Skok, Matrix Partners) is to ensure that the lifetime value of your customers exceeds the cost of customer acquisition by at least a factor of three.

It's hard to accurately calculate these at this stage, so instead, do a back-of-the-envelope calculation based on your people/hardware costs and subscription revenue to find your break-even point.

What About Freemium?

Freemium is a popular model used by numerous web applications. It was first popularized by Fred Wilson on his blog, where he described it as follows:

> *Give your service away for free, possibly ad supported but maybe not, acquire a lot of customers very efficiently through word of mouth, referral networks, organic search marketing, etc., then offer premium priced value added services or an enhanced version of your service to your customer base.*
>
> —Fred Wilson, AVC *blog*

On the surface, freemium seems like the best of both worlds: get users to try your service without having to worry about price, then up-sell them into the right premium plan later. But the reality is quite different.

First, I believe that unless you are deriving monetary value from free users, the freemium model is less of a business model and more of a marketing tactic to fill your pipeline with potential prospects.

Second, I believe pricing is one of the riskiest (and most critical) parts of the business model and should be tested early. Freemium delays this learning.

The Problems with Freemium

While I agree that freemium can be a highly effective model, I don't advocate starting with it for the following reasons:

Low or no conversions.

Many services make the mistake of giving away too much under their free plans, which leads to very low or no conversions. One reason for this is that creatives (artists, musicians, developers) are especially known to undervalue their own work and are really bad at setting pricing.

Pricing should be set with the buyer in mind, not the seller.

But the main reason is something we covered in the preceding section. You don't yet have enough usage data to correctly define the *free* plan so that users naturally outgrow it at some predictable time in the future.

Long validation cycle.

Even the best freemium services report conversion rates in the 0.5% to 5.0% range, which leads to long validation cycles. Time is the most valuable resource for a startup, and you can't afford such long learning cycles on something as critical as price.

Focus shifts to the wrong metric.

Because "free" can be irrationally appealing, freemium has a tendency to cause a premature shift in focus from user retention to user acquisition (signups). Unless you have built the right product, getting more signups is a form of waste. You don't need a lot of traffic to build the right product—just the right initial customers.

Your free users are not your customers (yet).

Low signal-to-noise ratio.

When you have a lot of free users, it's hard to focus your attention on the right feedback.

Given the opportunity, everyone can be a critic.

Free users aren't "free."

Even though the operational costs of carrying a free user may seem low, they aren't zero. In addition to server bandwidth/hosting costs, there are support, feature, and learning costs (like the ones described earlier) that need to be taken into account.

Lincoln Murphy described a quid pro quo test in his paper, "The Reality of Freemium in SaaS," for valuing free users. Unless free users are adding participatory value (as found in services with high network effects like LinkedIn, Facebook, and Twitter), they are an expense.

Jason Cohen, who writes the popular *A Smart Bear* blog, even advocates accounting for free users as a "marketing expense" on your balance sheet, much like you would an ad buy or trade show expense.

How to Approach Freemium

Here's how I approach freemium:

Start with the premium part of freemium first.

Once you recognize freemium as a marketing tactic and make a conscious decision to shorten the validation cycle, it makes sense to start with the premium part of freemium first and use a single pricing plan your customers will bear.

Since your eventual goal is to charge for your product anyway, why not start there? Pick features and a plan based on what customers will pay for today and sign them on as your first customers. Not only is this simpler to build, but it's also simpler to measure.

Then, once you have learned how your customers are using your product, you can always offer a free plan if you want to. You would have collected valuable usage data along the way, which puts you in the best position to design multiple upstream and downstream plans.

What is a good free plan?

A good free plan should ideally behave similarly to a free trial. The difference is that while a free trial is time-based, freemium is usage-based. If you understand the usage pattern of your product, you should be able to design the free plan so that a user naturally outgrows it at some point in the future that you can reasonably predict.

At that point, the difference between freemium and free trial is the perception of offering something free, which is a big enough difference to warrant the use of freemium for certain types of products.

When should you use freemium versus free trials?

Once you've built the right product, freemium can be a powerful user acquisition strategy for consumer-facing products that naturally tend to be more "free" driven.

Businesses, on the other hand, have come to expect time-based trials, and the added complexity of tracking and carrying free users may not be warranted here.

Build a Profitable Business First: MailChimp

MailChimp is frequently cited as one of the freemium model success stories, but too often people fail to recognize that MailChimp didn't start with a free plan. In fact, the company spent years building a powerful, affordable (but not free), profitable product first, with years of pricing experimentation, before backing into a free plan.

How to Build a Teaser Page

While there are a number of tactics for getting people to agree to an interview, you eventually have to be able to *attract unaware visitors and convert them into interested prospects.*

The number-one way to get a prospect (cold or warm) to agree to an interview is to "nail his problem."

One of the best exercises for crafting such a message involves spending an afternoon writing a shorter version of a long-form sales letter—no matter what type of business you're building.

You will not be sending this letter to any prospects. The point of the exercise is to get you to explain your product in narrative form, which will be helpful when requesting interviews, when conducting interviews, and while building a marketing landing page.

How to Write a Sales Letter

While there's more that goes into a complete sales letter, I recommend starting with just your unique value proposition (UVP), problem, and solution.

All you need for this exercise is a text editor. You can use different fonts, but avoid graphics at this stage and just focus on the copy.

Make a large promise (UVP).

This is a short headline that summarizes what your product will do for the customer (i.e., the finished story benefit).

A good formula we used earlier (by way of Dane Maxwell) is:

Instant Clarity Headline = End Result Customer Wants + Specific Period of Time + Address the Objections

Psychological principle in play: Attention through surprise, clarity, and bold promise.

Connect with the customer (Problem).

This is a short paragraph that explains the problem from the customer's worldview. You want to visualize the customer nodding his head in agreement. During your interviews, check for this.

Psychological principle in play: Empathy, by showing you understand the customer.

Generate interest/desire (Solution).

Then, state what your product does in another short paragraph (i.e., how it solves the problem) and list your top three features written as benefits.

Psychological principles in play: Interest and desire, by helping the customer visualize the solution and see how it ties to the main problem.

Refine your sales letter so that it flows.

The purpose of each sentence should be to get the next one read.

CASE STUDY

CloudFire: Sales Letter for Parents

Share all your photos and videos in less than five minutes.

Having kids creates a whole new appreciation for free time.

After kids, you probably find yourself taking a lot more photos and videos than before, but sharing all this content is time-consuming and sometimes painful. You have to organize, resize, and convert your files, and then babysit the upload process.

Like most other parents, you are probably sleep-deprived and don't have as much free time as before, and you would much rather spend your time doing other things.

CloudFire is a photo- and video-sharing service designed for parents by parents. It simplifies the sharing process so that you can go back to the more important things in your life.

Here are three reasons why you should use CloudFire:

- Instant gratification: You'll never have to wait on an upload again. Share your photos and videos instantly right from iPhoto or your desktop folders.
- Easy for you and your viewers: No registration or signup required to view your galleries.
- Safe, private, and secure: Password protection and 256-bit encryption keep prying eyes out. No ads or spam. Ever.

How to Create a Teaser Landing Page

With your sales letter in hand, if your product will have a website, you are now ready to put up a basic problem-focused teaser landing page. The main purpose of this landing page is to start testing your UVP and build a list of potential prospects you could interview.

Establishing a website early with the right keywords from your UVP will also give you a head start in building your search engine optimization (SEO) ranking. Don't worry about giving away too much about your product. We're only going to mention the "Problem," not the "Solution."

The key here is to start simple. You'll have ample time to refine this teaser page into a full-fledged marketing website later.

Here's how to get started:

Pick a product name.

>This is probably the hardest part of this exercise, mostly because it is so difficult to find .com domain names that aren't already taken. That being said, don't get too worked up over finding the right name. There are many examples of great companies with made-up names and vice versa. Sometimes simply brainstorming key words for your UVP might reveal a name that works:

>Lean Canvas: Business Model Canvas + Lean Startup

>USERcycle: User Lifecycle Management Software

Make sure the Twitter handle and Facebook page are available.

>If you are able to register the .com domain, you will more than likely be in the clear with everything else. Register them now, even if you don't intend to use them right away.

Keep it simple at first and just state your UVP.

>Your UVP will be one of the most important elements of your finished landing page, and it's all you need to put on a teaser page. The objective right now is to grab attention by articulating a problem that resonates with your visitors, not pitching your product.

Follow basic SEO practices.

>Make sure you also use your UVP in your title tag and place your keywords (not your product name) early.

>For example, use this:

>Customer Lifecycle Management Software – USERcycle

>not this:

>USERcycle – Customer Lifecycle Management Software

Don't fret over the logo yet.

>If you already have a logo or you can pull one together in a day, use it. Otherwise, skip it for now and use just your product name.

Collect email addresses.

>Pick your favorite tool, like Campaign Monitor or MailChimp, to collect email addresses using a "Notify Me" call-to-action button.

Measure your website.

>Start with a free analytics tool like Google Analytics to track visitors on your landing page.

How to Get Started with Continuous Deployment

Figure A-1 shows an overview of the continuous deployment cycle.

- SCM - GIT, SVN, CVS
- TRUNK STABLE

- SERVER MONITORING
- ALERTING

- UNIT TESTS
- FUNCTIONAL TEST
- CONTINUOUS INTEGRATION

- ONE-CLICK PUSH/ROLL BACK
- FEATURE FLIPPER SYSTEM

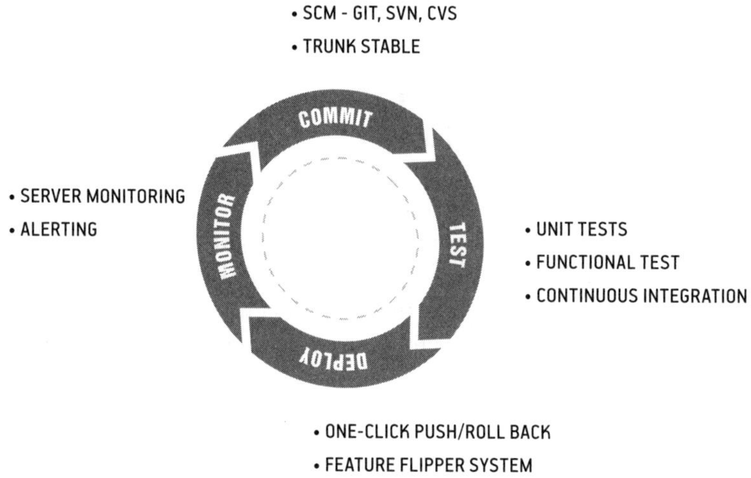

Figure A-1. *Continuous deployment cycle*

You probably already have (or should have) the pieces needed to put together a basic continuous deployment system.

I'll cover each stage of the continuous deployment cycle next.

Commit

One of the ways continuous deployment strives to reduce waste is by reducing work-in-progress inventory (i.e., undeployed code). Having lots of undeployed code increases inertia and reduces your ability to react quickly (more integration, more coordination, more planning).

Here are two techniques that help you reduce your work-in-progress inventory:

Code in smaller batches.

> The basic idea here is to deploy less code but more frequently. The definition of a small batch is relative, but strive to make it *as small as possible*. I used to deploy code on a biweekly schedule with my last product and eventually got my batch size down to the output of a two-hour coding session. Sure, you won't usually finish a full feature in two hours, but you'll get pretty good at building and deploying features incrementally.

The number of lines of code in my average batch went from several hundred to about 25. A direct side effect of deploying fewer than 25 lines of code versus hundreds is that troubleshooting unexpected production issues immediately after a deployment becomes a whole lot easier, as does fixing and releasing them.

Always be trunk-stable.

Another practice for reducing work-in-progress inventory is to not use any branching in your source control tree. I know this sounds a little extreme because branching and merging are among the most touted features in a source control management system—they allow you to isolate big, risky changes off the "stable" mainline trunk. But the longer you stay off the trunk, the more integration debt you collect, which again inevitably leads to more integration risk, coordination, and planning headaches.

It's more efficient to train yourself to always be trunk-stable and build and deploy your features incrementally. It's important to point out that deploying features incrementally doesn't necessarily mean they are made live to all users immediately. This allows you to incrementally roll out big features and make them available to select users like your internal team until you are ready to go live. I'll cover how you do this using a feature flipping system in the "Deploy" section.

Test

Taking the continuous deployment plunge is particularly scary because it eliminates manual testing (QA), which typically has served as a safety net for catching defects after development and before deployment.

Here are some guidelines for overcoming this fear:

Testing is everyone's responsibility.

First, I don't know of any two- or three-person startup that has a QA department, which makes testing everyone's responsibility. Second, having long test cycles creates the same work-in-progress inventory problems we discussed earlier. The solution is not creating a separate QA function, but rolling it into the development process and investing more heavily in automated testing.

Use a continuous integration server.

Set up a continuous integration server, like Hudson, to automatically trigger a build (if you have compiled code) and run your application against your test suite after every commit.

Do not tolerate any failing tests.

I've worked at places where developers train themselves to ignore failing tests because they know they are outdated. In a continuous deployment system, these tests serve as your last line of defense before pushing code into production, and you cannot tolerate a single failing test, especially since your ultimate goal is to automate deployment.

Prefer functional tests over unit tests.

I don't advocate achieving "full test coverage." On the contrary, I believe writing unit tests for obscure edge cases is a form of waste and is not the most optimal use of time when the focus is speed and learning. I instead prefer creating functional tests over unit tests whenever possible. There are several great options, like Selenium and Sauce Labs, for writing and automating functional tests for web applications.

Start with your activation flow.

Building tests for features that your customers never get to is also a form of waste. When building tests, use your customer lifecycle to prioritize your tests. Start with the activation flow and then incrementally add other functional tests over time.

Deploy

The deployment step pushes your tested code into your production environment. As this can get quite sophisticated when you have a cluster of machines, it is best to start early when you have just a few servers:

Outsource as much of your server infrastructure as possible.

Spending effort setting up and configuring your own servers at this stage is a form of waste. You should instead pick a cloud or platform provider (like Amazon or Heroku) and focus all your efforts on building your application, not your infrastructure.

Many cloud providers offer free tiers to get you started.

Create a separate staging area if you are so inclined.

A separate staging area serves as an additional safety net before pushing code to production and can be a good idea for building up confidence in your deployment system. However, I've found staging areas to be of limited use beyond basic spot checking, and at some point your continuous integration server should be able to serve this function in a more repeatable and automated fashion.

Build one-click push and rollback scripts.

The next step is to write a set of deploy scripts that can push your code to your production server and roll back your code to the last release. The rollback is used in the event you push a bad change. If you are deploying small enough batches, you should never need to roll back beyond the last release.

If you are on Heroku, one-click push and rollback is offered out of the box.

Deploy manually first, then automate.

It is usually a good idea to run the push script manually at first and audit every deployment while you build up your confidence. If you are using Hudson as your continuous integration tool, it is fairly easy to add a task to automatically trigger your push script when you are ready for that.

Implement a simple feature flipper system.

You will inevitably be faced with having to deploy a new "big" feature while maintaining the old ones, and you'll need a mechanism in place to isolate your users from these changes. A feature flipper system fits that bill.

A feature flipper system uses flags in your code that allow you to enable/disable features on a per-user basis.

Monitor

The job of your monitoring system is to enable you to automatically detect, alert, and eventually even automatically recover from unexpected errors. An example of recovering from an error might be automatically triggering your rollback script in the event of a bad release. To be able to do this, your monitoring system would have to get pretty sophisticated and not just monitor your server health but also your application health (i.e., business metrics).

The good news is that you don't need to start there. It is actually a form of waste to try to overbuild your monitoring system, because the Pareto Principle rules here.

The Pareto Principle: Roughly 80% of the effects come from 20% of the causes.

The continuous deployment cycle has a built-in feedback loop that helps you build this monitoring incrementally.

Here's how to get started:

Start with off-the-shelf monitoring.

There are numerous off-the-shelf monitoring and alerting applications, including Ganglia, Nagios, and New Relic, that you can use to start monitoring basic server health metrics.

Tolerate unexpected problems only once.

You build up your monitoring system by implementing a Five Whys root cause analysis to every unexpected problem you encounter.

The *Five Whys* is a questions-asking method used to explore the cause/effect relationships underlying a particular problem. Ultimately, the goal of applying the Five Whys method is to determine a root cause of a defect or problem.

The following example demonstrates the basic process:

My car will not start. (the problem)

Why? – The battery is dead. (first why)

Why? – The alternator is not functioning. (second why)

Why? – The alternator belt has broken. (third why)

Why? – The alternator belt was well beyond its useful service life and has never been replaced. (fourth why)

Why? – I have not been maintaining my car according to the recommended service schedule. (fifth why, a root cause)

Why? – Replacement parts are not available because of the extreme age of my vehicle. (sixth why, optional footnote)

I will start maintaining my car according to the recommended service schedule. (solution)

—http://en.wikipedia.org/wiki/5_Whys

Applied to unexpected problems in your production environment, the outcome of each Five Whys analysis should provide a slew of tests, monitoring, and alerts that you then add to your existing suite.

How to Build a Conversion Dashboard

A key design principle is to *decouple data collection from data visualization.*

This lets you minimize waste by allowing you to build your conversion dashboard incrementally.

How to Collect Data

Here's how to get started with data collection:

Map metrics to events.

The first step is to identify all the key events (user actions) that map back to your metrics. You should already have all your steps for your acquisition and activation funnels clearly defined (see Figure A-2).

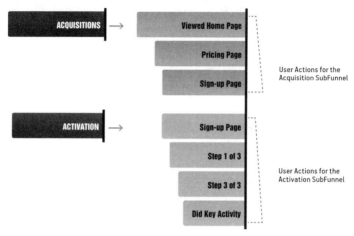

Figure A-2. *Mapping metrics to events*

It is helpful to also identify any key events for the other macro metrics (see Figure A-3).

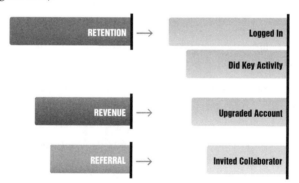

Figure A-3. *Other macro metrics*

Track raw events.

I recommend tracking your raw events in a separate events table/ database or using a third-party system like Google Analytics, KISSmetrics, or Mixpanel. While logging data in your production tables might seem easy and harmless enough, your production tables are probably not designed for the kinds of queries you'll need to run over time. You'll end up either spending a lot of time dumping tables and massaging the data, or taxing your production system heavily for reports.

Log everything.

A good practice to complement tracking raw events is to log every "potentially interesting" property along with each event. An example of a property could be your user's browser, operating system, or referrer. While you may not use a particular property today (or think you'll ever use it in the future), it's fairly inexpensive to log a few extra bytes of information that could end up saving you time later, and more important, could provide a treasure trove of historical data.

How to Visualize Your Conversion Dashboard

Now you're ready to start visualizing your data:

Build a weekly cohort report.

The first report I use on my conversion dashboard is the weekly cohort report by join date I showed earlier (see Figure A-4).

Conversion Funnel for June

June 1 Weekly Cohort	**June 8** Weekly Cohort	**June 15** Weekly Cohort	**June 22** Weekly Cohort
90 (70%) ACQUISITION	100 (71%) ACQUISITION	110 (70%) ACQUISITION	120 (69%) ACQUISITION
78 (87%) ACTIVATION	85 (85%) ACTIVATION	100 (91%) ACTIVATION	112 (93%) ACTIVATION
15 (19%) REVENUE	16 (19%) REVENUE	20 (20%) REVENUE	25 (22%) REVENUE

Figure A-4. *Weekly cohort report*

You'll notice that I base my activation conversion rate off the number of "acquired" users versus total visitors. This is because I like to measure my activation rate (signup flow efficiency) independently from my acquisition rate (marketing efficiency). This way, if you get a surge of unanticipated PR traffic (like getting Digg'd or TechCrunch'd), unless these visitors truly intend to use your service (i.e., click your signup link), they will not affect your overall activation numbers.

The weekly cohort report serves like a canary in a coal mine. If you find none of your numbers changing from week to week, you are simply spinning your wheels and not really making progress. A change in the numbers in a particular week lets you tie back those results to actions taken in that week.

Be able to drill into your subfunnels.

You should be able to drill into your detailed subfunnels and visualize all the steps, which is valuable for troubleshooting problems (see Figure A-5).

Activation Funnel for June

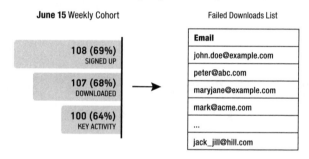

Figure A-5. *Activation funnel*

Be able to go behind the numbers.

At any given subfunnel event, you should be able to go behind the numbers and get to the list of people (see Figure A-6).

Figure A-6. *Going behind the numbers*

How to Track Retention

Retention measures repeated activity over a period of time. So the first step is to define what constitutes activity.

Define an active user.

There are many ways to define an active user. The most basic definition measures activity simply in terms of logins (i.e., does the user come back?).

A more representative definition for tracking activity for product/market fit should measure not just usage but also "representative usage." Every product has a core set of user actions that track ongoing representative usage. For example, writing blog posts is a key activity for a blogging platform. Also note that your key activity for activation may not be the same as your key activity for retention.

A more advanced approach to measuring representative engagement comes from Dharmesh Shah, who coined the term "Customer Happiness Index," or *CHI*. The idea is to use a formula to grade activity on a scale of 1 to 100 that is calculated using frequency, breadth, and depth of feature usage.

At this stage, I recommend starting with the simplest formula. This formula should measure representative engagement that centers around your key activity.

You can tweak the formula for your product over time to get a more graded CHI score that helps you segment your users into different buckets and focus your marketing, troubleshooting, and customer development activities.

CASE STUDY

CloudFire

The key activity in CloudFire that tracks ongoing usage is the sharing of content.

I would start by simply defining an active user as someone who shares at least one photo album or movie during the trial period (30 days).

A more advanced approach might be to calculate a Customer Happiness Index using a weighted formula similar to the following:

CHI = [(Number of days logged in)/(Desired number of logins)*0.2 + (At least one key activity) *0.8)] * 100

Then define an active user as someone with a CHI > 80. While this yields the same number of active users as before, it gives me a graded scale for segmenting my users by activity.

Figure A-7 shows what four users with varying levels of activity over the trial period would look like.

USER	LOGINS	KEY ACTIVITY	CHI	ACTIVE
A	20	2	93	Yes
B	10	1	87	Yes
C	5	0	3	No
D	15	0	10	No

Figure A-7. *Active users*

Visualize retention in your conversion dashboard.

Now that you have a definition of an active user, you can visualize your conversion dashboard to show what percentage of users were active during your trial period (see Figure A-8).

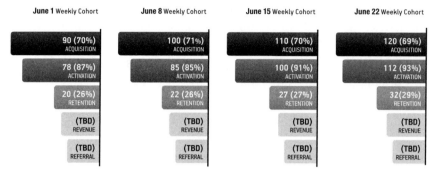

Figure A-8. *Visualizing retention*

The retention rate is based on the number of "activated" users.

Provide a detailed view.

As with your other macro metrics, drilling into the retention macro should provide a detailed view. However, in this case, instead of showing a subfunnel, you would show the trending of your retention numbers over time (see Figure A-9).

WEEK JOINED	1 MONTH LATER	2 MONTHS LATER	3 MONTHS LATER	4 MONTHS LATER	5 MONTHS LATER	6 MONTHS LATER	7 MONTHS LATER
JUN 1	26%	24%	22%	20%	20%	20%	20%
JUN 8	26%	25%	24%	22%	22%	22%	?
JUN 15	27%	26%	25%	23%	23%	?	
JUN 22	29%	27%	27%	25%	?		
JUN 29	32%	30%	30%	?			
...	...	...	...	...	...	...	...

Figure A-9. *Retention table*

NOTE ————————————————————————————————

You should ideally be able to change the time periods on both axes in Figure A-9, allowing you to visualize this report by day, week, or month.

Index

E

early adopters
  crossing chasm between mainstream customers and, 170
  homing in on, after Problem interviews, 90
  qualifying in Problem interviews, 86
  targeting in UVP, 30
early traction
  exit criteria, 159
  iterating toward and determining if you've achieved it, 159
  retention of 40% of activated users, 158
  Sean Ellis test for determining, 156
80/20 rule, 146
Ellis, Sean, 156
email addresses, collecting, 186
email reminders during customer trials, 138
emotional hook, on CloudFire landing page, 142
engines of growth
  identifying key engine of growth, 160
  tuning and resetting, 170
  viral engine of growth, 166
entrepreneurs as artists
  creative addiction and, 162
  curse of constantly reinventing themselves, 164
errors, catching and reporting in customer trials, 137
events (user actions), mapping metrics to, 192
exit criteria
  for Problem interviews, 91
  for Solution interviews, 108
experiments
  CloudFire landing pages, 143
  CloudFire MVP interview, 129
  defined, 11
  falsifiable hypotheses for Problem interviews, 83–84
  getting ready for, 57–68
    applying iteration meta-pattern to risks, 66–68
    assembling problem/solution team, 57–59
    communicating learning early and often, 64
    correlating results to specific actions, 64
  creating accessible dashboards, 64
  doing smallest thing possible to learn, 61
  formulating a falsifiable hypothesis, 62
  identifying single key metric or goal, 61
  maximizing for speed, learning, and focus, 59–61
  validating qualitatively and verifying quantitatively, 63
  iteration meta-pattern, 12
  systematic testing of business plan, 11
external funding, 10

F

Facebook, 165, 186
  beginnings of, 166
  validating value before growth, 167
features, 145–154
  adding or killing after Solution interviews, 108
  building and deploying incrementally, 188
  constraining your features pipeline, 147–149
  implementing 80/20 rule for prioritizing focus, 146
  lifecycle, 151–154
    process steps, 152
    tracking features on Kanban board, 151
  minimal marketable features (MMFs), 148
  processing feature requests, 149
  pulled, not pushed, 145
feedback, freemium users and, 182
feedback from customers, facilitating, 135
finished story benefits, 30
first-mover advantage, 42
Five Whys, questions to explore cause/effect relationships of a problem, 191
flow
  creating daily flow, 177
  creating weekly flow, 178
  definitions of, 177
focus groups, 71
  reasons not to substitute for customer interviews, 72

Have it your way.

Get even more for your money.

Join the O'Reilly Community, and register the O'Reilly books you own. It's free, and you'll get:

- $4.99 ebook upgrade offer
- 40% upgrade offer on O'Reilly print books
- Membership discounts on books and events
- Free lifetime updates to ebooks and videos
- Multiple ebook formats, DRM FREE
- Participation in the O'Reilly community
- Newsletters
- Account management
- 100% Satisfaction Guarantee

Signing up is easy:

1. **Go to: oreilly.com/go/register**
2. **Create an O'Reilly login.**
3. **Provide your address.**
4. **Register your books.**

Note: English-language books only

To order books online:
oreilly.com/store

For questions about products or an order:
orders@oreilly.com

To sign up to get topic-specific email announcements and/or news about upcoming books, conferences, special offers, and new technologies:
elists@oreilly.com

For technical questions about book content:
booktech@oreilly.com

To submit new book proposals to our editors:
proposals@oreilly.com

O'Reilly books are available in multiple DRM-free ebook formats. For more information:
oreilly.com/ebooks

O'REILLY®

Spreading the knowledge of innovators   oreilly.com